John Johonnot

Stories of Heroic Deeds

John Johonnot

Stories of Heroic Deeds

ISBN/EAN: 9783337331016

Printed in Europe, USA, Canada, Australia, Japan

Cover: Foto ©Thomas Meinert / pixelio.de

More available books at **www.hansebooks.com**

STORIES
OF HEROIC DEEDS

FOR BOYS AND GIRLS

BY

JAMES JOHONNOT

NEW YORK ❧ CINCINNATI ∴ CHICAGO
AMERICAN BOOK COMPANY

PREFACE.

In preparing this little book, three things have been kept constantly in mind—the plan of the whole series, the thought and sentiment expressed in each lesson, and the language used to express the thought.

The main feature of the plan is to furnish pupils interesting historical stories for the purpose of giving them a taste for the study of history, to enable them to distinguish between fact and fiction, and to stimulate them to high endeavor by noble example.

In selecting, preparing, and arranging the stories, care has been taken that the thought is such as to be readily understood, and that on the whole it tends to awaken the higher emotions. The moral lesson involved should be absorbed rather than learned, and the teacher should beware of destroying the value of any lesson by dealing out moral pap.

The language is that of common life, such as the pupil hears every day from parent, friend, and teacher—such as the morning newspaper brings, and such as is necessary for him to master in its printed and written forms in the shortest possible time. When a word is unknown, the teacher should develop its meaning before permitting the lesson to go on. The interest in the story will be a sufficient stimulus to secure the best of attention, and the highest excellence in delivery.

In the use of language, it is far better that pupils should be obliged to stretch upward rather than be remanded to the nursery. Baby-talk should no more be revived than long-clothes, and the time spent in writing stories in words of one syllable might be used to a much better purpose.

The history of the Do-as-you-likes speaks for itself. It is a fancy story rather than a myth, but it is one that children will like, long before they will understand its whole significance; and we much doubt whether the Rev. Charles Kingsley ever produced a more valuable and original book than " Water-Babies," from which this story is taken.

CONTENTS.

MYTHS.

INDIAN STORIES.

STORIES OF THE REVOLUTION.

SCOTTISH STORIES.

MISCELLANEOUS STORIES.

MYTHS.

I.—*LATONA AND THE RUSTICS.*

1. ONCE on a time the goddess Latona wandered into the country with her infant twins in her arms. Weary with her burden and parched with thirst, she espied in the bottom of the valley a pond of clear water, where the country people were at work gathering willows and osiers. The goddess approached, and, kneeling on the banks, would have slaked her thirst in the cool water but the rustics forbade her.

2. "Why do you refuse me water?" said she; "water is free to all. Nature allows no one to claim as property the sunshine, the air, and the water; I come to take my share of the common blessing. Yet I ask it of you as a favor. I only desire to quench my thirst. My mouth is so dry that I can hardly speak. A draught of water would revive me, and I would own myself in-

debted to you for life itself. Let these infants move your pity, who stretch out their little arms as if to plead for me."

3. Who would not have been moved with the gentle words of the goddess? But these clowns would not desist; they even added jeers and threats of violence if she did not leave the place. Nor was this all; they waded into the pond, and stirred up the mud with their feet, so as to make it unfit to drink.

4. Latona was so angry that she lifted up her voice to Heaven and cried out, "May they never quit that pool, but pass their lives there!" And so it came to pass. They now live in the water, sometimes below and sometimes with their heads above the surface. Sometimes they come out on the bank, but soon leap again into the water. They still use their bass voices in railing, and, though they have the water all to themselves, they still croak about it. Their voices are harsh, their throats bloated, their mouths have stretched, their necks have disappeared, and their heads are joined directly to their bodies. Their backs are green, their huge bellies white, and they leap instead of walking. Have you seen anything like them?

II.—THE MUSIC OF PAN.

1. PAN, the earth-god, had great skill in music, and he performed upon his pipes in a wonderful way. Everybody praised him, and he grew so vain that he thought no one could equal him, and he sent a challenge to Apollo, the god of the lyre, to a trial of skill. The challenge was accepted, and Imolus, the mountain-god, was chosen um-pire. Imolus cleared away the trees from his ears, to listen. At a given signal, Pan blew his pipes, and his rustic melody greatly pleased himself and his followers.

2. Then Imolus turned his head toward the sun-god, and all the trees turned with him. Apol-lo rose: in his left hand he held the lyre, and with his right hand struck the strings. The music was truly heavenly, and Imolus at once awarded the victory to the god of the lyre. All agreed with him except old King Midas, who happened to be present. He questioned the decision of the umpire, and declared that Pan's music was the best. Apollo would not permit such a depraved pair of ears any longer to wear the human form, but caused them to grow out long, and to become hairy within and without, and movable at the

roots. So the old king, as long as he lived, wore
the ears of a donkey.

----♦----

III.—BAUCIS AND PHILEMON.

1. ON a certain hill in Phrygia stand a linden-
tree and an oak. Not far from the spot are a marsh,
and a lake which was once the site of a thriving
village. Once on a time, Jupiter, in human shape,
and Mercury, without his wings, paid a visit to
this country, and, after a weary day's walk, they
reached the village about nightfall. Here they
applied for shelter in vain. Everywhere they
were driven away with insults, and even, in some
places, the dogs were set upon them. At last they
reached the outskirts of the village, where stood
a humble thatched cottage. Here Baucis, a pious
old dame, and her husband Philemon, united when
young, had grown old together.

2. One need not look here for master or for
servant; they two were the whole household, master and servant alike. Here the two travelers
found rest. As they crossed the humble threshold, and bowed their heads to pass under the low

door, the old man placed a seat, and Baucis set
about preparing them some food. She raked out
the coals, kindled up the fire with dry sticks, and
with her scanty breath blew it into a flame. Her
husband gathered pot-herbs from the garden, and
cut a slice of bacon from the flitch in the chimney,
which Baucis quickly prepared for the pot. She
then filled a beechen bowl with clean water for her
guests to wash, keeping up a pleasant talk all the
time.

3. On the bench where her guests were to sit
she placed a cushion filled with sea-weed, and then
set out the table. This she rubbed down with
sweet-smelling herbs, and placed upon it some
olives, radishes, and cheese, and eggs lightly cooked
in the ashes. All was served in coarse earthen
dishes. When all was ready, the stew, smoking
hot, was placed upon the table. Some wine was
added; and, for dessert, apples and wild-honey;
and, over and above all, friendly faces and simple
and hearty welcome.

4. The guests sat down, and the old couple saw
with astonishment that, as fast as it was poured
out, the wine renewed itself, and they then knew
that they were entertaining superior beings. They
begged pardon for the coarseness of their fare, but

Jove raised them to their feet, thanked them for
their kindness, and then said : "We are gods.
The people of the village must pay the penalty
for their indolence and cruelty. Come with us to
the top of yonder hill." They hastened to obey,
and, with staff in hand, labored up the steep ascent.
At the top they turned their eyes below, and they
saw the whole village turned into a lake, and their
house the only one remaining.

5. But, while they gazed with wonder at the
sight, their old cottage changed into a temple. Lofty columns took the place of the corner-posts, the
thatch was changed to a gilded roof, the floors became marble, and the doors were hung with orna-
ments of gold. Then Jupiter spoke and said :
"Excellent old people, what favors have you to
ask of us ? " Then Baucis and Philemon took
counsel together, and answered, " Let us finish
our lives here, where we have lived so long, and
we wish to pass from life together in the same
hour."

6. The prayer was granted. For many years
they were the keepers of the temple, and when
they were very old, as they stood before the steps
of the sacred edifice, they felt themselves stiffen
so they could not stir. At the same moment a

leafy crown grew over the heads of each, and they
had scarcely time to say, " Good-by, dear Philemon,"
" Good-by, dear Baucis," when they were changed
into two stately trees—he into a sturdy oak, and
she into a graceful linden. There they stand, side
by side, to the present day, and when the wind
rises the peasant can hear the rustle of the leaves
as the branches caress each other, which seems to
say, " Dear Baucis ! " " Dear Philemon ! "

IV.—THE DRAGON'S TEETH.

1. For many years Cadmus traveled in search
of his lost sister Europa, who was carried off by
Jupiter in the disguise of a white bull. As he
was unsuccessful, he dare not return to his own
country, but consulted the oracle to know where
he should settle. He was told to follow a cow,
and where she lay down he should found a city
and call it Thebes. As he came out of the cave
where the oracle dwelt, he saw the cow and followed her. After several hours' weary tramp she
lay down on a broad plain, and Cadmus saw that
here he must build his city.

2. He gave thanks, and, wishing to offer a sacrifice to Jupiter, he sent his servants to bring pure water for a libation from a grove near by. In the cave by the fountain lurked a horrid serpent with a crested head, and scales glittering like gold. His eyes shone like fire, and he had a triple tongue and triple rows of teeth. No sooner had the servants dipped their vessels in the water, than out rushed the serpent with a fearful hiss and killed them all with his fangs and poisonous breath.

3. Cadmus waited until midday for their return, and then went in search of them. He wore a lion's hide, and besides his javelin he carried a lance. When he entered the wood and saw the dead bodies of his men, and the monster with his bloody jaws, he exclaimed, "O faithful friends, I will avenge you or share your death!" So saying, he lifted a huge stone and threw it at the serpent, but it made no impression on the monster. Cadmus next threw his javelin, and this penetrated the serpent's scales. Fierce with pain, the monster broke off the handle of the weapon but left the iron point still in the flesh. His neck swelled with rage, bloody foam covered his jaws, and the breath of his nostrils poisoned the air around. Now he threw himself forward upon Cadmus, but

the hero retreated backward holding his spear before the monster's open jaws. At last Cadmus
made a sudden thrust with the spear and pinned
the serpent's head to a tree. Then how the monster did writhe, and hiss, and spit out his venom!
but the spear held fast, and he soon died.

4. Then Cadmus heard a voice telling him to
take out the dragon's teeth and sow them in the
ground. So he made a furrow in the ground, and
into it he sowed the teeth and covered them up.
Scarce had he done so, when the clods began to
move, and the points of spears appeared above the
ground. Next helmets, with their nodding plumes,
came up, and next the shoulders and breasts and
limbs of men. Soon a crop of warriors stood before him, all armed for fight. Their looks became
fierce and cruel as they stood and glared at one
another. Cadmus was afraid of his life, but one of
them said, "Meddle not with our civil war." At
length one of the warriors raised his sword and
smote down another. Then commenced a fight,
and soon all of them were killed but five. These
cast away their weapons and said, "Let us live in
peace." They joined Cadmus, and helped him
build his city of Thebes.

V.—THE DO-AS-YOU-LIKES.

1. THE fairy brought out from her cupboard a big book, and Tom and little Ellie read in the title-page, " The History of the Great and Famous Nation of the Do-as-you-likes, who came away from the Country of Hardwork, because they wanted to play on the Jew's-harp all day long."

2. In the first picture they saw these Do-as-you-likes living in the land of Ready-made, at the foot of the Happy-go-lucky Mountains, where flap - doodle grows wild ; and if you want to know what that is, you must read "Peter Simple."

3. Instead of houses, they lived in the beautiful caves of tufa, and bathed in the warm springs three times a day ; and, as for clothes, it was so warm there that the gentlemen walked about in little besides a cocked hat and a pair of straps, or some light summer tackle of that kind ; and the ladies all gathered gossamer in autumn to make their winter dresses.

4. They were very fond of music, but it was too much trouble to learn to play the piano or violin ; so they sat on ant-hills all day long and played on the Jew's-harp; and if the ants bit

them, why they just got up and went to the next
ant-hill, till they were bitten there also.

5. And they sat under the flapdoodle-trees,
and let the flapdoodle drop into their mouths;
and under the vines, and squeezed the grape-juice
down their throats; and if any little pigs ran
about ready roasted, crying "Come, and eat me,"
as was the fashion in that country, they waited
till the pigs ran against their mouths, and then
took a bite, and were content, just as so many oys-
ters would have been.

6. They needed no weapons, for no enemies
ever came near their land; and the stern old fairy
Necessity never came near them to hunt them up,
and make them use their wits or die. And so on,
till there were never such comfortable, easy-going,
happy-go-lucky people in the world.

7. "Well, that is a jolly life," said Tom. "You
think so?" said the fairy. "Do you see that great
peaked mountain there behind, with smoke coming
out of its top?" "Yes." "And do you see those
ashes, and slag, and cinders lying about?" "Yes."
"Then turn over the next five hundred years, and
you will see what happens."

8. And behold! the mountain had blown up like
a barrel of gunpowder, and then boiled over like

a kettle ; whereby one third of the Do-as-you-likes were blown into the air, and another third were smothered in the ashes ; so that there were only one third left. "You see," said the fairy, "what comes of living on a burning mountain."

9. "Oh, why did you not warn them?" said little Ellie. "I did warn them all I could. I let the smoke come out of the mountain, and wherever there is smoke there is a fire. And laid the ashes and cinders all about ; and wherever there are cinders, cinders may be again. But they did not like to face facts, my dears, as few people do ; and so they invented a cock-and-bull story, which, I am sure, I never told them, that the smoke was the breath of a giant, whom some god or other had buried under the mountain ; and other nonsense of that kind. And when folks are in that humor I can not teach them, save by the good old birch-rod."

10. And then she turned over the next five hundred years ; and there were the remnant of the Do-as-you-likes, doing as they liked, as before. They were too lazy to move away from the mountain ; so they said, "If it has blown up once, that is all the more reason it will not blow up again." And they were few in number, but they only

said, "The more the merrier, but the fewer the better fare."

11. However, that was not quite true; for all the flapdoodle-trees were killed by the volcano, and they had eaten all the roast pigs, who, of course, could not be expected to have little ones; so they had to live very hard, on nuts and roots which they scratched out of the ground. Some of them talked of sowing corn, as their ancestors used to do, before they came into the land of Ready-made, but they had forgotten how to make plows, and had eaten all the seed-corn which they had brought out of the land of Hardwork years since; and of course it was too much trouble to go away and find more. So they lived miserably on roots and nuts, and all the weakly little children had great stomachs, and then died."

12. "Why," said Tom, "they are growing no better than savages." "And look how ugly they are all getting!" said Ellie. "Yes; when people live on poor vegetables, instead of roast beef and plum-pudding, their jaws grow larger and their lips grow coarser, like the poor people who eat nothing but potatoes."

13. And she turned over the next five hundred years, and there they were all living up in trees,

and making nests to keep off the rain. And underneath the trees lions were prowling about.
" Why," said Ellie, " the lions seem to have eaten
a good many of them, for there are very few left
now ! " " Yes," said the fairy, " you see it was only
the strongest and most active ones who could climb
the trees, and so escape." " But what great, hulk-
ing, broad-shouldered chaps they are ! " said Tom ;
" they are as rough a lot as ever I saw."

14. And she turned over the next five hundred
years. And in that they were fewer still, and
stronger, and fiercer; but their feet had changed
shape very oddly, for they laid hold of the branches
with their great-toes, as if they had been thumbs,
just as a Hindoo tailor uses his toes to thread his
needle.

15. The children were very much surprised,
and asked the fairy whether that was her doing.
" Yes and no," she said, smiling. " It was only
those who could use their feet as well as their
hands who could get a good living; so they got
the best of everything, and starved out all the
rest." " But there is a hairy one among them,"
said Ellie. " Ah ! " said the fairy, " that will be
a great man in his time, and chief of all the tribe."

16. And when she turned over the next five

hundred years, it was true. For this hairy chief had hairier children still. The climate was growing so damp that none but the hairy ones could live; all the rest coughed and sneezed, and had sore throats, and went into consumptions, before they could grow up into men and women.

17. Then the fairy turned over the next five hundred years. And they were fewer still. "Why, there is one on the ground picking up roots," said Ellie, "and he can not walk upright." No more he could; for, in the same way that the shape of their feet had altered, the shape of their backs had altered too. "Why," said Tom, "I declare they are all apes!"

18. "Something fearfully like it, poor, foolish creatures," said the fairy. "They are grown so stupid now, that they can hardly think; for none of them have used their wits for many hundred years. They have almost forgotten, too, how to talk. For each stupid child forgot some of the words it heard from its stupid parents, and had not wit enough to make fresh words for itself. Besides, they have grown so fierce and suspicious and brutal, that they keep out of each other's way, and mope and sulk in dark forests, never hearing each other's voice, till they have forgotten almost

what speech is like.   I am afraid they will all be
apes very soon, and all be doing only what they
liked."

19. And in the next five hundred years they
were all dead and gone, by bad food and wild
beasts and hunters ; all except one tremendous old
fellow with jaws like a jack, who stood full seven
feet high ; and M. du Chaillu came up to him and
shot him, as he stood roaring and thumping his
breast.   And he remembered that his ancestors
had once been men, and he tried to say, " Am I
not a man and a brother ? " but he had forgotten
how to use his tongue ; and then he had tried to
call for a doctor, but he had forgotten the word
for one.   So all he said was "Ubboboo !" and
died.   And that was the end of the great and
jolly nation of the Do-as-you-likes.

INDIAN STORIES.

VI.—COLUMBUS AND THE ECLIPSE.

1. WHEN Columbus first landed upon the shores of the New World, and for a long time after, the natives thought that he had come down from heaven, and they were ready to do anything for this new friend. But, at one place, where he stayed for some months, the chiefs became jealous of him and tried to drive him away. It had been their custom to bring food for him and his companions every morning; but now the amount they brought was very small, and Columbus saw that he would soon be starved unless he could make a change.

2. Now, Columbus knew that in a few days there was to be an eclipse of the sun; so he called the chiefs around him and told them that the Great Spirit was angry with them for not doing as they agreed in bringing him provisions, and

that, to show his anger, on such a day, he would cause the sun to be darkened. The Indians listened, but they did not believe Columbus, and there was a still greater falling off in the amount of the food sent in.

3. On the morning of the day set, the sun rose clear and bright, and the Indians shook their heads, as they thought how Columbus had tried to deceive them. Hour after hour passed, and still the sun was bright; and the Spaniards began to fear that the Indians would attack them soon, as they seemed fully convinced that Columbus had deceived them. But at length a black shadow began to steal over the face of the sun. Little by little the light faded, and darkness spread over the land.

4. The Indians saw that Columbus had told them the truth. They saw that they had offended the Great Spirit, and that he had sent a dreadful monster to swallow the sun. They could see the jaws of this horrible monster slowly closing to shut off their light forever. Frantic with fear, they filled the air with cries and shrieks. Some fell prostrate before Columbus and entreated his help; some rushed off and soon returned laden with every kind of provisions they could lay their

hands on. Columbus then retired to his tent, and promised to save them if possible. About the time for the eclipse to pass away, he came out and told them that the Great Spirit had pardoned them this time, and he would soon drive away the monster from the sun ; but they must never offend in that way again.

5. The Indians promised, and waited. As the sun began to come out from the shadow, their fears subsided, and, when it shone clear once more, their joy knew no bounds. They leaped, they danced, and they sang. They thought Columbus was a god, and, while he remained on the island, the Spaniards had all the provisions they needed.

VII.—THE PEQUOTS.

1. EARLY in 1621 the Pilgrims who settled at Plymouth, Massachusetts, made a treaty with Massasoit, the chief of the Wampanoags, who inhabited the eastern part of the State. This treaty was observed by all the Indian tribes in the vicinity for a long time, and it was not until three years

after the first settlers arrived in Connecticut that
an Indian war broke out.

2. The Pequots were a small but very warlike tribe, living upon Long Island Sound, near
the border of Rhode Island. These Indians attacked the settlers, and in 1627 they killed three
men at Saybrook, and six men and three women
at Wethersfield.

3. These things caused great alarm, and a
council was called at Hartford to consider what
was to be done. A force, consisting of ninety
white men and seventy friendly Indians, under
the command of Captain Mason, were sent against
them.

4. They went down the Connecticut River
from Hartford to Saybrook in boats, and thence
eastward along the Sound to the Indian fort
Mystic, near where Stonington now stands. They
reached the spot about daybreak. The Pequots
had no suspicion that an enemy was near. But
as they reached the fort a dog barked, and the
Indian sentinel called out, "Owanux! Owanux!"
(Englishmen! Englishmen!), and the savages
sprang to arms. The soldiers fired and killed
many Indians, but it was a fight of the little army
of whites against six hundred.

5. The Indians fought bravely, and Captain Mason, fearful of being defeated, called out, " We must burn them ! " A torch was applied to a wigwam, and soon the whole fort was in flames. Seventy wigwams were burned, and six hundred men, women, and children perished.

6. A few Indians escaped, and, joining others of their tribe, took refuge in a swamp in Fairfield. Here the whites pursued them, and killed and captured nearly the whole tribe. The prisoners and all that remained alive of the Pequots, were divided and given to the Mohicans and the Narragansetts, two tribes friendly to the English.

VIII.—SCHENECTADY.

1. In the winter of 1690 a small party of French and Indians made a raid upon Albany. They concluded to destroy Schenectady first. The people of Schenectady had been warned of their danger, but they would not believe that men would come from Canada, a distance of two or three hundred miles, through the deep snows of winter, to molest them.

2. But they were fatally deceived. A strong stockade, of more than a mile in length, was built around the houses which composed the village. This stockade had a gateway at each end, and these gateways were usually carefully guarded at night. But, believing themselves safe, the watchman became careless and went to sleep. The enemy arrived on Saturday night, and succeeded in getting within the stockade without giving any alarm. They divided themselves into small parties, so that every house might be attacked at the same instant. They entered the place about eleven o'clock.

3. The inhabitants were all asleep, and stillness rested upon the place. With a noiseless step the enemy distributed themselves through the village, and, at a given signal, the savage war-whoop was sounded. What a dreadful cry was this to the startled fathers and mothers of this unhappy town !

4. It is scarcely possible to describe the scene that followed. The people, conscious of their danger, sprang from their beds, but were met at the door and slaughtered by the savages; and the Indians, rendered frantic by the wild scene, ran through the place, slaying those they chanced to meet.

5. Sixty of the people were killed, and twenty-five were made prisoners. Some attempted to escape, but as they were in their night-clothes, and the night was very cold, only a part of them reached Albany, sixteen miles distant, the nearest point of refuge, and of these, twenty-five lost limbs by the cold. As the alarm was given, the Indians returned to Canada without an attack upon Albany.

IX.---THE STORY OF MRS. DUSTIN.

1. In the winter of 1696 a party of Indians made an attack upon the town of Haverhill, Massachusetts. Among the people of that town was a Mr. Dustin. He was in a field at work, when the news of the attack reached his ears. He immediately started and ran to his house to save his family. He had seven children, and these he collected for the purpose of taking them to a place of safety before the Indians should arrive.

2. His wife was ill, and she had an infant but a week old. He now hurried to her, but, before she could get ready to leave the house, Mr. Dustin saw that a party of savages were already

8

close by. Expecting that all would be slain, he ran to the door and mounted his horse, with the intention of taking one of his children—the one that he loved best—and flying with it to a place of safety.

3. But which should he take? Which of his seven children should he leave to the savages? He could not decide, and therefore, telling the children to run forward, he placed himself between them and the Indians. The Indians fired at him, but they did not hit him. He had a gun, too, and he fired back at them.

4. Then he hurried his little children along, loading his gun as he went, and firing at his pursuers. Thus he proceeded for more than a mile—protecting his little family, defending himself, and keeping the enemy at a distance. At length, he reached a place of safety, where the children were beyond the reach of the Indians. His feelings were divided between joy for the escape, and grief for the poor wife left behind.

5. But Mrs. Dustin was destined to undergo the severest trials. Although she was very ill, the savages compelled her, with the nurse and her little infant, to go with them. They soon left the town of Haverhill, and set out to go to the homes

of the Indians. These were at a distance of one hundred and fifty miles. It was winter, and the journey was to be taken on foot through the wilderness.

6. Mrs. Dustin and the nurse were soon overcome with fatigue. The Indians, seeing that the little infant occupied much of their attention, snatched it from its mother, and killed the little innocent by striking it against a tree. After a toilsome march, and the greatest suffering, Mrs. Dustin and her companion completed the journey.

7. But now the Indians were to remove to a distant place, and these two women were forced to accompany them. When they reached the end of their journey, they found out that they were to be tortured. They then resolved to make their escape.

8. One night Mrs. Dustin, the nurse, and another woman rose secretly while the Indians were asleep. There were ten of them in the wigwam where they were. These the women killed with their own hands and then departed. After wandering a long time in the woods, they reached Haverhill, and Mrs. Dustin was restored to her family.

X.—ROGERS'S SLIDE.

1. MAJOR ROGERS, a brave patriot, commanded a corps of rangers in the winter of 1758. He was stationed on Lake George. One day he started with a few men to spy out the position of his Indian foes.

2. A band of Indians surprised the party, and put them to flight. Major Rogers, by the aid of his snow-shoes, was able to gain the summit of a hill overlooking the lake. At this point the lake is narrow, and the rocks are piled up in huge masses. One crag rises to the height of about four hundred feet, with an almost perpendicular surface, sloping down to the lake below.

3. The major knew that the Indians would follow rapidly on his track. When he reached the brow of the cliff he quickly cast off his knapsack and haversack, and sent them sliding down the icy path. He then took off his snow-shoes, and, without moving them, turned himself about and put them on his feet again. He retreated along the brow of the hill for several rods, and down a ravine he made his way to the lake, found his pack, and fled on the ice to Fort George.

4. The Indians arrived at the spot, saw the

Roger's Slide, Lake George.

two tracks, and supposed that two people had cast themselves off the rock rather than be captured. Just then they saw the bold ranger making his way across the ice, and believed that he had safely slid down the steep face of the rock. They thought that the pale-face must be protected by the Great Spirit, and made no attempt at pursuit. The rock has ever since been known as Rogers's Slide.

XI.—GENERAL CLINTON'S MARCH.

1. In the War of the Revolution, the Indians belonging to the Six Nations, living in Central and Western New York, mostly joined the British. For several years parties of Tories and Indians, every little while, would attack the frontier settlements and murder the settlers. In 1778 General Sullivan was sent into the country around Seneca Lake to break up the hostile force, and, if possible, to drive the Indians out of the country. A part of this force, under the American General Clinton, started from the Mohawk Valley to join Sullivan in Southern New York.

2. The march was through an unbroken wil-

derness. As there were no roads, their provisions were loaded into boats and floated up the small streams, and there the freight, boats, and all, were carried by the men to the head-waters of another stream. They had little trouble until they reached Otsego Lake, and from this point they expected less, as the outlet of the lake formed the Susque-hanna River, and on this river, far below, they expected to join Sullivan. But the weather was hot, and for many weeks there had been no rain. The river had not water enough to float the boats, and for a time Clinton thought he would be obliged to turn back.

3. But at last he hit upon a scheme that promised success. He built a dam across the river just where it flows out of the lake. His soldiers rolled in great bowlders from the fields, and filled the spaces between with brush and clay. The water could not flow out freely, and the lake began to rise. In three weeks it was six feet above its summer level. The boats were then made ready, with the provisions and men on board, and the dam was torn down. The waters flooded the banks of the narrow stream, and the whole party were carried down to the place of meeting with Sullivan in safety.

4. The Indians along the stream saw this sudden rise of waters, and they were much frightened. No rain had fallen, and the only way they could account for it was that the Great Spirit had sent the waters to help the white men, and they everywhere fled in the greatest alarm. General Clinton

did not meet one armed enemy until he joined Sullivan, and the combined army met no opposition until they reached the spot where Elmira now stands. Here a battle took place, in which the Indians were defeated. Upon the return of Sullivan from his successful raid into the Indian country, he was obliged to kill his horses for want of forage, and the place where the horses' skulls lay for a long time has since been called Horse-heads.

XII.—FRANCES SLOCUM.

1. In 1778 the Tories and Indians made an attack upon the little settlement of Wyoming, on the Susquehanna River, in Pennsylvania. The fort was captured, and nearly all the prisoners— men, women, and children — were murdered in cold blood. Every house was burned, and the few people who escaped into the woods, went through terrible trials before they reached a place of safety. Most of the savages had bloody scalps hung to their belts, to show that they had taken part in the battle and the murder that fol-lowed.

2. Near the scene of the Wyoming battle lived a Quaker, named Slocum, who had been a great

friend of the Indians. For a time no one troubled him; but early one morning some Indians came down, scalped a boy, named Kingsley, and carried away Frances, Mrs. Slocum's little daughter, five years old. Soon after, Mr. Slocum was also mur- dered. The mother stayed in the valley, hoping to hear of her lost child. When peace came, two brothers of the lost one went to Canada in search of her, but all their inquiries were in vain, and they gave her up as dead.

3. But the mother still hoped on. She was certain that Frances was still alive. Other cap- tives were found, but the mother went down to her grave without any tidings of the child that had been so cruelly taken from her. The broth- ers became aged men, and little Frances was al- most forgotten.

4. In 1837, fifty-nine years after her capture, an Indian agent and trader gave an account of a white woman living with the Indians near Lo- gansport, Indiana. Joseph Slocum and a sister at once set out for Ohio, where they met their younger brother, Isaac. The three then went on to Logansport, where they learned that the white woman lived about twelve miles distant. She was sent for, and the next morning she came rid-

ing into town upon a spirited young horse, and accompanied by her two daughters. She could not speak English, and an interpreter was found. She listened to what her brothers had to say, but did not answer. At sunset she started for her home, but promised to be back in the morning.

5. She came, true to her promise. The mother had told Joseph years before of one sure test. When they were little children Joseph, then a child two and a half years old, while playing with a hammer gave Frances a blow upon the middle finger of the left hand, which crushed the bone and deprived the finger of the nail. When Joseph told this incident the aged woman was greatly agitated, and, while tears streamed down her face, she held out the wounded finger. There was no longer a doubt. The love for her kindred which had slept for more than fifty years was aroused, and she eagerly inquired after her father, mother, brothers, and sisters.

6. Her full heart was opened, and she freely gave the story of her life. She said the savages took her to a cave in the mountains the first night. She was kindly treated, and was tenderly carried in their arms when she was weary. She was adopted by an Indian family, and brought up as their

daughter. For years she had led a roving life, and she liked it. She was taught the use of the bow, and soon learned all the arts of the Indian household. When she grew up, her Indian parents died, and she soon afterward married a young chief of the nation.

7. She was treated with more respect than Indian women generally are; and she was so happy in her life that the greatest evil she feared was that she should be obliged to go back to the whites, whom she regarded as the Indians' worst enemies. Her husband was dead, and she had been a widow many years. Children and grand-children were around her, and life was passing pleasantly away. When she finished her story, she lifted her right hand in a solemn manner and said, "All this is as true as that there is a Great Spirit in the heavens!"

8. The next day her brothers and sister went out to visit her at her home. She was living in a well-built log-house, which was surrounded by cultivated fields. She had a large herd of cattle and sixty horses. She had saved her share of the annuity which the Government paid the Indians, and had about one thousand dollars in specie. Her white friends stayed with her several days,

and had a delightful visit. Afterward Joseph, his wife, and daughter paid her another visit, and then bade her a last farewell. She died about 1844, and was buried with great honors, as she was regarded as a queen by her tribe.

XIII.—OBED'S PUMPKINS.

1. MOVING was serious business ninety years ago, when the Moore family migrated to Ohio, for everything had to be carried hundreds of miles in a wagon, and there was no sending back for anything forgotten. So Obed prudently secured passage for some pumpkin-seeds, lest a failure of pumpkin-pies for Thanksgiving might annul that festival altogether in the unknown wilderness.

2. There was only one room in their new house, and no regular up-stairs at all—only a loft where the boys slept, and to which they had to climb on a ladder when they went to bed. Ruth and Dolly slept in the trundle-bed down-stairs.

3. That first winter was a hard one, but nobody really suffered. Mr. Moore was clearing up his land, so they had an abundance of fuel; the boys

trapped rabbits, and their father's musket kept
them supplied with other game, but Mrs. Moore
had to measure the flour and meal very carefully,
and as for other things, they went without, only
once, when Obed found a squirrel's nest in a hollow tree, and came in with his pockets full of
nuts.

4. "Little did that rascal know who he was
gathering these for," he remarked, as they cracked
them on the hearth that evening. "Yes, and may-
be it's little you know who you'll raise your pumpkins for. Injuns, like as not," said Joe.

5. One morning Dolly declared that she had
been wakened in the night by mice in the chimney-
cupboard. "It *can't* be mice; we're too far from
neighbors," said Mrs. Moore, opening the cupboard.
Joe climbed upon a chair behind her, and there
on the topmost shelf were some nibbled scraps of
cloth and paper.

6. "O Obed!" he exclaimed, in dismay,
"your pumpkin-seeds are all gone!" Just then
there was a rustle, and he caught sight of two
bright, black eyes. They saw him, too, and
another rustle gave him a vanishing glimpse of a
bushy tail. "It's squirrels!" he shouted; "Obed,
they've come to get their pay for the nuts you

stole." "Oh, dear!" said Obed, "I'd rather have my pumpkin-seeds than all the nuts that ever grew. We never shall taste pumpkin-pies again, now."

7. Weeks afterward they were burning out some stumps in the clearing, when out from a hollow one popped a squirrel. Obed ran to investigate, and, poking around and pulling away the rotten wood, brought to light some rags and bits of paper. "Hello!" he exclaimed, "the identical chap that carried off my pumpkin-seeds!" And sure enough, there were the empty shells, and among them—oh, for a vision of the smile that lighted Obed's freckled face!—three whole, sound seeds.

8. All their crops did well that first year, and the way those pumpkin-vines bore was a marvel; but no abundance could shake Obed's resolve to reserve the first pumpkin-pies for Thanksgiving.

9. On the preceding Monday, Mr. Moore started for the nearest village to purchase winter supplies. With many brave assurances and secret misgivings, his family saw him set out, for the journey required two days, and the Indians were growing threatening of late. But when the first night had worn away in safety, they began to feel easier, and gave themselves up to the Thanksgiving preparations.

10. "O Obed!" said Joe, as late in the after-
noon he staggered into the house under a huge
yellow pumpkin, "let's make some jack-lanterns;
'twon't hurt the pumpkins for pies." Obed as-
sented, and they had just completed those gro-
tesque horrors, and were going out to do the
chores, when a man galloped up, and everybody
rushed to the door.

11. "Get ready for the redskins!" he shouted,
springing from the saddle, "and give me a fresh
horse. They killed a family down the river last
night, and nobody knows where they'll turn up
next! Husband away? Whew! that's bad!
Well, shut up as tight as you can. Cover up
your fire, and don't strike a light to-night." And,
leaping upon the horse the boys led around, he
flew away to warn the next settler.

12. They made what hasty preparations they
were able, and Mrs. Moore reluctantly yielded to
Obed's urgent plea that she would keep the
younger children quiet in the loft, while he and
Joe watched below.

13. The two boys crouched beside the hearth
listening to every sound. At last Obed crept to
the window. A snow-flurry had whitened the
ground early in the evening, and, as he peered out,

the boy descried shadows moving across the fields. "They're coming, Joe!" he whispered; "stand by that window with the axe, while I get the rifle pointed at this one."

14. Joe noiselessly stationed himself, and Obed opened the bullet-pouch. As his fingers came in contact with the leaden balls, his heart chilled. They were too large for his rifle! They belonged to the musket, and his father had taken the wrong pouch. With a last despairing hope he was feeling in the cupboard for any chance balls that might have been left behind, when he stumbled over something that nearly threw him headlong. It was the forgotten jack-lantern. With a sudden thought he pulled off his coat and flung it over the face of the lantern, then searching in the ashes for a live coal, cautiously lighted the candle within and closed the opening. With every sense sharpened to its utmost, he lifted the pumpkin and went softly toward the window. Ten or twelve dusky figures were stealthily nearing the house, and at the same instant he detected a slight noise at the door.

15. "They'll sound the war-whoop in a minute, if I give them time," he said to himself. "Now for it!" And he dropped the coat, leaving the

grinning monster exposed to view.   Mrs. Moore,
listening with bated breath in the room above,

just then heard an unearthly yell, and fainted
dead away. "Quick, Joe! Light up the other
one!" exclaimed Obed, excitedly, as he saw the
savages flying wildly back to the woods.

16. Joe, with every hair on end, was still standing valiantly at his post, his uplifted axe ready to
fall on the first head that should risk an entrance.
He had paid no attention to Obed's movements,

and was momentarily expecting to hear the roar of the old rifle.

17. "The other jack-lantern! Don't you see that's what scar't 'em so?" demanded Obed as, emboldened by his success, he bobbed the hideous thing up and down before the window. Joe finally comprehended, and, speedily lighting the second one, imitated Obed's lively evolutions with such effect that, when Mrs. Moore came-to, the yells were dying away in the distance, and she heard Obed climbing the ladder.

18. The anxious mother now gathered her family in the room below, and watched patiently for daylight and her husband. They came together, and the story had to be told all over again. "And so," added Joe, "Obed did raise his pumpkins for the Injuns, after all."

XIV.—THE GASPE.

1. JUST before the Revolution, the British ship-of-war Gaspé was sent to Narragansett Bay to see that the trade was all right there. Lieutenant Duddington was the commander, and he annoyed the traders as much as possible. He would order a vessel to stop, go on board of her, and, having seen that everything was right, would go off with words of insult instead of apology. The Governor of Rhode Island ordered Duddington to let the trading-vessels alone, but the pert little officer only laughed at him. Next the Governor appealed to Admiral Watson, and received an insulting reply.

2. By this time the people were aroused. The petty little tyrant had issued an order that all vessels sailing up the bay should lower their flag by way of salute—an order very much like that of Gessler when he required the people to bow to

a hat set upon a post. On the 9th of June Captain Lindsay, coming up in his packet, refused to lower his flag. The Gaspé gave chase, but Captain Lindsay dodged about among the shoals in such a way that the Gaspé got aground on the sand. Here she must stick until high tide, about three o'clock the next morning.

3. The news soon reached Providence. Mr. John Brown, one of the leading merchants, saw that it was a good time to end the troubles. He fitted out eight of the largest boats he could get, and placed them under the command of Captain Whipple, one of his most trusted ship-masters. The boats left Providence about ten o'clock in the evening, with sixty-four men, armed with paving-stones. As they approached the Gaspé, the sentinel hailed them, and Lieutenant Duddington fired a pistol at them. The reply was a single musket-shot, which brought the officer down, badly wounded. The ship's company were then ordered ashore, and the ship set on fire. At dawn she blew up.

4. A large reward was offered by Admiral Watson for the discovery of the parties engaged in this affair. Although the boats were publicly fitted out, and their departure was seen by hun-

dreds of people, not one jot of information could he get. Commissioners sent over from England met with no better success, and after a trial of six months they gave it up as a bad job. A poem, written in regard to this affair, concludes with this verse:

5. "Now, for to find these people out,
   King George has offered very stout:
   One thousand pounds to find out one
   That wounded William Duddington;
   One thousand more he says he'll spare
   For those who say the sheriffs were;
   One thousand more there doth remain
   For to find out the leader's name;
   Likewise five hundred pounds per man
   For any one of all the clan.
   But let him try his utmost skill,
   I'm apt to think he never will
   Find out any of those hearts of gold,
   Though he should offer fifty-fold."

XV.—ETHAN ALLEN.

1. DURING the Revolution, the pride and the hero of the Green Mountains was Ethan Allen, and probably there was no man living then that had more of the elements of the popular hero than he. He was tall, almost a giant in stature, and strong in proportion. He was easily excited to anger, and his rage was something terrific. In another place it is told how he surprised and captured the strong fortresses of Ticonderoga and Crown Point. Afterward he was captured and taken prisoner to England. The brutal British officer in command put him in irons, and one day spat in his face. Allen, beside himself with rage at this insult, with his teeth wrenched off the head of the nail which fastened his handcuffs, and attacked the officer, who was obliged to retreat to save his life.

2. With all his rough ways and fits of anger Allen was a remarkably honest man. It is related of him that he owed a person in Boston sixty pounds, for which he gave his note. When due, it was sent to Vermont for collection. Allen could not pay at the time, and he employed a lawyer to postpone the payment until he could raise the

money. The lawyer arose in court and denied Allen's signature to the note, as this would oblige the other party to send to Boston for a witness, and give Allen all the time he wanted.

3. When the lawyer made his plea, Allen, who happened to be in the back part of the court-room, strode forward, and in a voice of thunder addressed the lawyer: "Mr. Jones, I did not hire you to come here to lie! This is a true note—I signed it—I'll swear to it—and I'll pay it! I want no shuffling, I want time. What I employed you for was to get this matter put over to the next court, not to come here and lie and juggle about it." The lawyer shrank from his blazing eye, and the case was put over as he wished.

XVI.—JOSEPH REED.

1. A HERO of another kind, and one we should never forget, is Joseph Reed, of New Jersey. He entered the patriot army, and proved a brave and efficient officer. In 1778 he entered Congress, and, while quiet, he became one of the most useful members. Soon after he entered Congress, a Brit-

ish commission was sent out to see if the difficulties between the two countries could not be adjusted and the war terminated. The terms they offered, however, did not include independence. Convinced that they could not accomplish their object directly, the commissioners resorted to deceit and bribery, and they offered Joseph Reed ten thousand guineas if he would use his influence to help along their project. The noble patriot heard the offer with great indignation, and replied, "I am not worth purchasing, but, such as I am, the King of Great Britain is not rich enough to buy me." The poet Freneau has recorded this incident in a poem from which the following extract is made :

2. " No single art engaged his manly mind,
      In every scene his active genius shined ;
      Nature in him, in honor to our age,
      At once composed the soldier and the sage.

3. " Firm in his purpose, vigilant and bold,
      Detesting traitors, and despising gold,
      He scorned all bribes from Britain's hostile
         throne,
      For all his country's wrongs were thrice his
         own."

XVII.—GENERAL PRESCOTT.

1. In 1777 the British troops upon the Island of Rhode Island were commanded by General Prescott. Of all the disreputable officers sent over by the British during the Revolution, he was the meanest and the worst. He was cruel at heart, a petty tyrant, and a real coward. His government was so offensive to the people of Rhode Island, that they determined to put an end to it. The British army was stationed at Newport, and the British ships sailed up and down Narragansett Bay to protect the island from any attempted surprise on the part of the Americans. Feeling perfectly secure under the protection of the fleet, General Prescott made his headquarters at the house of a Mr. Ovington, five miles out of Newport, and beyond the British military lines.

2. The residence of General Prescott became known to the patriot leaders at Providence, and they resolved to make an effort to capture him. The enterprise was intrusted to Colonel William Barton, who entered upon the service with zeal and discretion. On the night of July 10, 1777, Barton, with a few chosen men, embarked in four whale-boats, and with muffled oars rowed

across the bay to the island, passing directly through the fleet of ships and guard-boats. They came so near the ships that they could hear the sentinel's cry of "All is well!" After landing they made their way silently to the Ovington house, and captured the guard without creating an alarm.

3. Barton boldly entered the house, and found Mr. Ovington reading, the rest of the family being in bed. He inquired for General Prescott's room, and was told it was directly overhead. Taking with him four sailors, and Sisson, a powerful negro, Barton ascended the stairs, and gently tried the door. It was locked; but there was no time to be lost: the negro drew back a few paces, and, using his head for a battering-ram, burst open the door at the first effort. Prescott begged time to dress, but, as time was precious, he was hurried down to the shore without clothes, and placed in the boat, where he could dress at leisure. The boats then took their way back in perfect silence, and about midnight landed upon the mainland in safety. "Sir, you have made a bold push to-night!" said Prescott, to his captor. "We have been fortunate," replied Barton.

XVIII.—PRESCOTT AND THE YANKEE BOY.

1. IN the spring of 1778, Prescott was ex-
changed for General Charles Lee, and returned to
Rhode Island. Soon afterward the British admiral invited the general to dine with him and his
officers on board his ship, then lying in front of
Newport. Martial law yet prevailed on the island,
and men and boys were frequently sent by the
authorities on shore to be confined in the ship as
a punishment for slight offenses. There were several on board at the time.

2. After dinner, the free use of wine made the
company hilarious, and toasts and songs were frequently called for. A lieutenant remarked to the
admiral, "There is a Yankee lad confined below
who can shame any of us in singing."

3. "Bring him up," said the admiral. "Yes,
bring him up," said Prescott. The boy was
brought to the cabin. He was pale and slender,
and about thirteen years of age. Abashed by the
presence of great officers, with their glittering uni-
forms, he timidly approached, when the admiral,
seeing his embarrassment, spoke kindly to him,
and asked him to sing a song.

4. "I can't sing any but Yankee songs," said

the trembling boy. "Come, my little fellow, don't be afraid," said the admiral. "Sing one of your Yankee songs—any one you can recollect."

5. The boy still hesitated, when the brutal Prescott, who was a stranger to the lad, roared out: "Sing us a song, or I will give you a dozen with the cat!" But the admiral interfered and told him to sing, and he should be set at liberty the next morning. Thus encouraged, the lad sang the following ballad, composed by a sailor at Newport:

6. " 'Twas on a dark and stormy night,
    The wind and waves did roar ;
    Bold Barton then, with twenty men,
    Went down upon the shore.

7. " And in a whale-boat they set off,
    To Rhode Island fair,
    To catch a red-coat general
    Who then resided there.

8. " Through British fleets and guard-boats strong
    They held their dangerous way,
    Till they arrived unto their port,
    And then did not delay.

9. " A tawny son of Afric's race
    Them through the ravine led,
    And entering then the Overton house,
    They found him in his bed.

10. " But to get in they had no means
    Except poor Cuffie's head,
    Who beat the door down, then rushed in.
    And seized him in his bed.

11. " 'Stop ! let me put my clothing on,'
    The general then did pray ;
    'Your clothing, massa, I will take,
    For dress we can not stay.'

12. "Then through rye-stubble him they led,
      With shoes and clothing none,
    And placed him in their boat quite snug,
    And from the shore were gone.

13. "Soon the alarm was sounded loud,
      'The Yankees they have come,
    And stolen Prescott from his bed,
      And him have carried home!'

14. "The drums were beat, sky-rockets flew,
      The soldiers shouldered arms,
    And marched around the ground they knew,
      Filled with most dire alarms.

15. "But through the fleet with muffled oars
      They held their devious way,
    And landed him on 'Gansett shores,
      Where Britons held no sway.

16. "When unto land the captors came,
      When rescue there was none,
    'A bold push this,' the general cried;
      'Of prisoners I am one.'"

17. The boy was frequently interrupted by
roars of laughter at Prescott's expense, which
strengthened the child's nerves and voice; and
when he had concluded his song, "I thought,"

wrote a gentleman who was present, "the deck would go through with the stamping." General Prescott joined heartily in the merriment produced by the song, and, thrusting his hand into his pocket, he pulled out a coin, and handed it to the boy, saying, "Here, you young dog, is a guinea for you!" The boy was set at liberty the next morning, and went ashore.

<hr>

XIX.—BATTLE OF THE KEGS.

1. In 1777, while the British occupied Philadelphia, Washington made an effort to destroy their shipping. He caused torpedoes to be constructed in the form of strong kegs, and launched in the river, hoping that the tide would float them against the British ships, when they would explode. But the British discovered them, and for a time were greatly frightened. Then they opened upon them a furious cannonade; and for the next twenty-four hours they fired at everything that floated in the water. Mr. Hopkinson, the author of "Hail, Columbia," has given the the following amusing account of this battle:

2. Gallants attend, and hear a friend
   Trill forth harmonious ditty;
Strange things I'll tell, which late befell
   In Philadelphia city.

3. 'Twas early day, as poets say,
   Just when the sun was rising,
A soldier stood on log of wood,
   And saw a sight surprising.

4. As in his maze, he stood to gaze,
   The truth can't be denied, sir,
He spied a score of kegs or more
   Come driving down the tide, sir.

5. A sailor too, in jerkin blue,
   The strange appearance viewing,
First rubbed his eyes in great surprise,
   Then said, "Some mischief's brewing."

6. The soldier flew, the sailor too,
   And, scared almost to death, sir
Wore out their shoes to spread the news,
   And ran till out of breath, sir.

7. Now up and down, throughout the town,
   Most frantic scenes were acted ;
And some ran here, and others there,
   Like men almost distracted.

5

8. Some fire cried, which some denied,
    But said the earth had quakèd;
 And girls and boys, with hideous noise,
    Ran through the streets half naked.

9. Now in a fright, Howe starts upright,
    Awaked by such a clatter;
 He rubs both eyes, and boldly cries,
    "For God's sake, what's the matter?"

10. At his bedside he then espied
    Sir Erskine at command, sir;
 Upon one foot he had one boot,
    And 'tother in his hand, sir.

11. "Arise! arise!" Sir Erskine cries,
    "The rebels—more's the pity—
 Without a boat, are all afloat,
    And ranged before the city!

12. "The motley crew, on vessels new,
    With Satan for their guide, sir,
 Packed up in bags, or wooden kegs,
    Come driving down the tide, sir.

13. "Therefore prepare for bloody war!
    These kegs must all be routed;
 Or surely we despised shall be,
    And British valor doubted."

14. The royal band, now ready stand,
    All ranged in dread array, sir;
With stomach stout, to see it out,
    And make a bloody day, sir.

15. The cannons roar from shore to shore,
    The small-arms loud did rattle;
Since war began, I'm sure no man
    E'er saw so strange a battle.

16. The rebel dales, the rebel vales,
    With rebel trees surrounded,
The distant woods, the hills and floods,
    With rebel echoes sounded.

17. The kegs, 'tis said, though strongly made
    Of rebel stones and hoops, sir,
Could not oppose their powerful foes,
    The conquering British troops, sir.

18. From morn till night, these men of might
    Displayed amazing courage;
And, when the sun was fairly down,
    Retired to sup their porridge.

19. Such feats did they perform that day,
    Against those wicked kegs, sir,
That years to come, if they get home,
    They'll make their boasts and brags, sir.

XX.—THE DARING OF PAUL JONES.

1. It was in the spring of 1778 that the name
of John Paul Jones became so terrible along the
western coasts of Britain—his native coasts, as
familiar to him as to a Solway fisherman.

2. And what a tough, valiant, intractable, au-
dacious hero he was, with his foppish ways and
costume, his romantic, fantastic courtesy and en-
thusiasm! He had been a Nelson, if he had had
Nelson's opportunities. He was a little man, too,
like Nelson, though compactly built, and his voice
was "soft and still, and small, and his eye had
keenness and softness in it, and, full as he was of
the spirit of mastery, he was all gentleness, con-
sideration, generosity, to men who obeyed him."
Like all the greatest fighters, he performed his immortal exploits while he was young; he was but
thirty-two when he did his greatest day's work.

3. On the southwestern coast of Scotland John
Paul Jones was born. Nothing could keep him
from the sea. At twelve he was apprenticed to a
merchant in the American trade, in whose ships
he served seven years, as cabin-boy, and sailor before the mast. At the age of twenty-four we find
him settled in Tobago, engaged in commerce, and

possessing considerable property. In 1774 he came to the colonies. The Revolution breaking out, he obtained a lieutenant's commission in the forming navy of the United States. He acquired sudden and very great distinction. In one short cruise he took sixteen prizes, of which he burned eight and sent in eight. He had some sharp actions with king's ships, and captured one, which had on board a company of British troops, and ten thousand suits of clothes—a most precious acquisition in 1776.

4. It was Paul Jones who first hoisted the Stars and Stripes. On the very day, June 14, 1777, on which Congress resolved that "the flag of the thirteen United States be thirteen stars, white in a blue field, representing a new constellation," they also resolved that "Captain Paul Jones be appointed to command the ship Ranger." As he had been the first to hoist the flag of the United States on a ship-of-war, so, on entering the harbor of Brest in February, 1778, seven days after the signing of the treaty of alliance, he was the first naval officer who had the pleasure of acknowledging a salute to that flag from a foreign power.

5. Soon after, Captain Jones sailed in the Ranger for the Scottish coast, on his first cruise

in British waters. On the seventh day he was
between the Isle of Man and Whitehaven waters, which he knew as familiarly as New-Yorkers
do the Narrows. Whitehaven was the town at
which he had been apprenticed, and from which
he had sailed for ten years. It was a town of several thousand inhabitants, and its harbor con-
tained three or four hundred vessels closely moored
together. Jones had formed the daring scheme
of running in near the port, landing two parties,
burning all these ships, and retiring before an
armed force could be raised to repel him.

6. At midnight, with two boats and thirty-one
men, provided with combustibles and dark-lan-
terns, he left his ship and made for Whitehaven
pier. Day was dawning when he reached it, for
the light wind had made him hours too late in
starting. He would not abandon the enterprise,
however, unpromising as it seemed. Sending one
boat to the north side of the harbor to fire the
vessels collected there, he went himself to do the
same office to the stranded fleet on the south side.

7. Familiar with every foot of the ground he
had to traverse, he boldly landed under the guns
of the two forts that protected the harbor, and
he himself climbed the wall of one of them, and

spiked every gun, without giving alarm. All the
sentinels, he found, had gone to the guard-house,
and there he secured and disarmed every one of
them without giving or receiving a scratch. Then,
accompanied by one man, he scaled the other fort
and spiked its guns. Returning to the pier to be-
gin the conflagration, he found there the other boat,
which had come back for a light, the candles in
the lanterns having burned out. Jones now discovered that all his own candles were consumed,
and there was not in either boat a spark of fire, or
the means of kindling one. The day, too, had
dawned, and every second was precious. Nevertheless, he sent one of his men to a house near by
for a light, who soon returned successful, and the
boats again separated for the work of destruction.

8. Ten minutes later a barrel of fat, ignited
in the steerage of a ship that lay surrounded by a
hundred and fifty others, all left high and dry
by the receded tide, shot a bolt of roaring flame
through the hatchway. The people of the town,
in hundreds, were soon running to the pier. Captain Jones stood by the side of the burning vessel,
pistol in hand, and ordered the crowd to keep
their distance, which they did. Not till the flames
had caught the rigging and wreathed about the

mainmast, not till the sun was an hour high, not till the whole town was rushing amazed to the scene, did Jones give the order to embark.

9. His men entered the boats without opposition, the captain releasing, at the last moment, all his prisoners but three, who were all he had room for. He stood on the pier till his men were seated in the boats, and for some little time after; then, stepping gracefully into his place, he gave the word, the oars splashed into the water, and they moved toward the ship, while from every eminence in the vicinity hundreds and thousands of silent, astonished spectators gazed upon the unearthly scene.

10. "To the forts!" was the cry on shore, as soon as the spell of the enemy's presence was removed. "Their disappointment," says Jones, "may easily be imagined, when they found at least thirty heavy cannon, the instruments of their vengeance, rendered useless! At length, however, they began to fire, having, as I apprehend, either brought down ship-guns, or used one or two cannon which lay on the beach dismounted, and had not been spiked. They fired with no direction, and the shot falling short of the boats, instead of doing us any damage, afforded some diversion,

which my people could not help showing, by dis-
charging their pistols in return for the salute."
The people of the town succeeded in confining the
ravages of the fire to a few ships. Had it been
possible, he remarks, to have landed a few hours
sooner, he could have burned three hundred vessels.

XXI.—FORT MOULTRIE.

1. EARLY in 1776 Governor Rutledge, of South
Carolina, built Fort Moultrie, to protect Charles-
ton from an attack by sea. The fort was built
of palmetto-wood, which is soft, but very tough
and springy. In the middle of the fort was a low
place scooped out of the earth, designed to hold
water. Before the fort was finished, the British
admiral, Sir Peter Parker, with two large ships-
of-war, made his appearance off the harbor. Colonel Moultrie commanded within the fort. His
men were all militia, and had never been in battle
before.

2. Sir Peter commenced a furious attack upon
the fort from his principal ships. But the balls
entered the soft palmetto-wood and did no dam-

age. Shells were thrown into the fort, struck in
the interior ditch, which on the day of battle was
filled with mud, instead of water, and the fuses
were put out, or the shells burst and did no other
damage than covering the men with a thick coat
of mud. All day long the ships kept up their
terrible broadsides, and all day long did the brave
militiamen in the fort return the fire slowly but
with good aim. It would not do to waste fire, as
powder was low ; and several times during the
battle the gunners were obliged to stop firing until a new supply of powder came in from the city.

3. In the meantime, the people in the city
were fearful and anxious ; that small, half-fin-
ished fort was all that stood between them and
capture. They could hardly believe that Colonel
Moultrie with his raw troops could resist the attack of a formidable British fleet. All day long
they heard the boom of the cannon, and all day
long the steeples and roofs of houses were crowded
with anxious spectators. With joy, they saw the
ships crawl away toward night, fearfully cut
up, while the fort continued its firing as the
powder came slowly in. Then the bells rang,
and a shout went up, that cheered the hearts of
the brave garrison at the fort. One of the ships

got aground, and was set on fire and burned up
Only ten of the militia were killed, and twenty,
two wounded, while the loss on the ships num-
bered hundreds.

4. One incident of this battle is worthy of
note. During the action, the flag-staff was shot

away, and the flag fell to the earth outside the
fort. Sergeant William Jasper at once jumped
over the parapet, picked up the flag, and, amid the
storm of iron from the fleet, he fastened it to a
staff and set it up once more, and then leaped

unhurt into the fort. The next morning Governor
Rutledge publicly thanked Jasper, and gave him a
small sword that hung by his side. Three years
later the gallant sergeant was killed in the attack
upon Savannah.

XXII.—COUNT PULASKI AND HIS BANNER.

1. COUNT CASIMER PULASKI was a native of
Poland. At an early age he entered the army,
where he soon became a leader of a patriotic movement to rid Poland at once of an unpopular king
and of Russian rule. His little army was defeated,
and in 1771 he entered the service of the Turks,
then at war with Russia. In 1776 he went to
Paris and had an interview with Dr. Franklin,
and resolved to enter the service of the United
States. He sailed for America the next year, and
was placed by Washington in command of cavalry.
He proved a very valuable acquisition to the
American cause. His familiarity with military
affairs enabled him to bring his corps to a high
degree of efficiency in regard to discipline, and in
battle he was a very thunderbolt. He was stationed along the New Jersey coast, keeping watch

of the British during the greater part of 1778; and the next spring he was ordered south to assist General Lincoln and the Count d'Estaing in the reduction of Savannah.

2. This enterprise, planned by Washington with every prospect of success, met with a series of mishaps and disasters from the very first. The troops were tardy in concentrating, enabling the British commander to complete measures of defense which at first were very imperfect. Then there was a want of co-operation between the American forces and their French allies. When everything was in readiness, Count d'Estaing granted the British commander twenty-four hours truce, which he employed to so good a purpose that the idea of an assault was abandoned, and the operations were turned into a siege. For twelve days there was constant battle, ending in a general assault. No troops ever fought better, but they were driven back from the strong fortifications of the enemy with great loss. The golden moment was lost, and the great sacrifice of life was in vain. Count Pulaski was in the van of the fight during all these anxious days, and was stricken down at the very last moment, a hero dying for our freedom.

3. In 1777 Pulaski visited Lafayette while
that officer was wounded, and under the care of
the Moravian nuns, at Bethlehem, Pennsylvania.
When it became known that the brave Pole was
raising a company of cavalry, the nuns prepared a
banner of crimson silk, beautifully wrought with
the needle by their own hands, and sent it to
Pulaski with their blessing. This banner he received with grateful thanks, and took it with him
in every battle to the day of his death.   The story
of this banner is beautifully told by Longfellow:

4. " When the dying flame of day
    Through the chancel shot its ray,
    Far the gleaming tapers shed
    Faint light on the cowlèd head;
    And the censer burning swung, '
    When before the altar hung
    That proud banner, which with prayer
    Had been consecrated there;
And the nuns' sweet hymn was heard the while.
Sung low in the dim, mysterious aisle.

5. " Take thy banner.   May it wave
    Proudly o'er the good and brave,
    When the battle's distant wail
    Breaks the Sabbath of our vale;

When the clarion's music thrills
To the hearts of these lone hills;
When the spear in conflict shakes,
And the strong lance, shivering, breaks

6. "Take thy banner; and, beneath
The war-cloud's encircling wreath,
Guard it—till our homes are free—
Guard it—God will prosper thee!
In the dark and trying hour,
In the breaking forth of power,
In the rush of steeds and men,
His right hand will shield thee then.

7. "Take thy banner. But when night
Closes round the ghastly fight,
If the vanquished warrior bow,
Spare him—by our holy vow;
By our prayers and many tears;
By the mercy that endears—
Spare him—he our love hath shared;
Spare him as thou wouldst be spared.

8. "Take thy banner, and, if e'er
Thou shouldst press the soldier's bier,
And the muffled drums should beat
To the tread of mournful feet,

Then this common flag shall be
Martial cloak and shroud for thee.
And the warrior took that banner proud,
And it was his martial cloak and shroud."

XXIII.—LYDIA DARRAH.

1. WHILE the British were in Philadelphia,
one of Howe's principal officers made his quarters
at the house of a Quaker named William Darrah.
His wife, Lydia, was a true patriot, but she said
so little, and performed her household work so
well, that she won the entire confidence of her
guest.   One day he said to her, "I expect some
friends to call this evening, and they will stay late,
so have your family out of the way early."   This
order aroused her curiosity, and, when her family
were in bed, she took off her shoes and went into
the passage and listened to what was going on.
She heard one of the officers read an order of Sir
William Howe for the troops to march out the
next night silently, and surprise Washington in
his quarters.   She went back to bed, and, when it
was time for her to get up and let out the visitors,

she was apparently fast asleep. She formed her plans during the night, and, early in the morning, she awakened her husband and told him that flour was wanted for family use, and that she must go to Frankford to get it.

2. It was a cold morning in December, and a deep snow covered the ground. On foot, with a bag in her hand, she set out, calling at Howe's headquarters for a permit to leave the city. At an early hour she reached Frankford, and, leaving her bag at the mill, she went on until she reached the American outposts. Here she met Colonel Craig, who had been sent out by Washington to get what news he could of the enemy. To him Mrs. Darrah told her story, and then went back to the mill, shouldered her flour, and hastened home.

3. From her window, the next night, in the cold starlight, she watched the British troops as they marched silently out of town, and a few hours later she saw them on their way back from their "fool's errand." The officer came home and bade Lydia go to his room. With an air of great secrecy he said, "Were any of your family up on the night when I had company in my room?" "No," she replied; "they all retired at eight

6

o'clock." "It is very strange," said the officer. "You, I know, was asleep, for I knocked on your door three times before you heard me. But, by some means, our plans became known, for, when we went out, we found Washington ready to receive us, with his cannon mounted and his troops under arms, so we were compelled to march back like a parcel of fools."

XXIV.—THE LIBERTY-BELL.

1. The old State-House at Philadelphia still stands, and is preserved with the greatest care. Thousands of people from all parts of the United States visit it every year, for here Congress met in 1776, and here the Declaration of Independence was signed, July 4th. In the State-House is kept the old Liberty-Bell, which is thought almost as sacred as the house itself.

2. This bell was bought in England, in 1752, for the State-House. It was then the largest bell in America. Upon the first trial-ringing it cracked, and it hung unused in the steeple for a year. It was then taken down and recast, with these words

in relief letters around its top: "*Proclaim liberty
throughout the land, unto all the inhabitants there-*

of." In the hall un-
derneath this very
bell, twelve years
later, Congress did
indeed proclaim lib-
erty, and the joyful ringing of this bell first told
the crowd of anxious people without that the
Declaration of Independence had been passed.

For two hours the tones of the bell floated down
from above and mingled with the roll of drums,
the booming of cannon, and shouts of the multitudes below.

3. After more than fifty years of service, the
bell was cracked again, and rendered useless. It
is now kept as a sacred relic of the past. The
following is the last stanza of a poem upon the
old bell by William Ross Wallace:

4. " That old bell is still seen by the patriot's eye,
    And he blesses it ever, when journeying by;
    Long years have passed o'er it, and yet every
        soul
    Will thrill, in the night, to its wonderful roll;
    For it speaks to its belfry when kissed by the
        blast,
    Like a glory-breathed tone from the mystical
        past.
    Long years shall roll o'er it, and yet every
        chime
    Shall unceasingly tell of an era sublime;
    Oh, yes! if the flame on our altars should
        pale,
        Let its voice but be heard, and the freeman
        will start,

To rekindle the fire, while he sees on the gale
All the stars and the stripes of the flag of
his heart."

XXV.—THE TORY'S HORSE.

1. WHILE Cornwallis was virtually master of
the Carolinas, raids were made in all directions to
prevent the patriots from assembling, and to break
up the bands of Sumter and Marion, which had
proved to be very annoying to the British commander. The most noted commander of these
raids was Colonel Tarleton, who displayed great
activity in plundering and burning the homes of
the patriots. Some of the planters were Tories,
and eagerly welcomed the British troops.

2. While Tarleton was out on one of his raids,
Macdonald, a young Scotchman, one of Marion's
men, played a curious trick on an old Tory, who
lived in the neighborhood. As soon as he heard
that Colonel Tarleton had encamped, he dressed
himself in the British uniform, and early in the
morning called upon the Tory, and said to him:

3. "Colonel Tarleton sends his compliments,

and, knowing you to be a good friend of the king, begs you will send him one of your best horses for a charger, to help drive the rebels out of the country."

4. "Send him one of my finest horses!" cried the old Tory, his eyes sparkling with joy. "Yes, Mr. Sergeant, that I will. A good friend of the king did he call me? Yes, God save his sacred majesty, a good friend I am, indeed, and true! And faith I am glad, too, that the colonel knows it. Here, Dick, run, jump, fly, you rascal, to the stable, and bring me out Selim. Young Selim! Do you hear?"

5. Then, turning to Macdonald, he went on: "Well, Mr. Sergeant, you have made me con- founded glad this morning, you may depend! And now, suppose you take a glass of peach—of good old peach, Mr. Sergeant? Do you think it would do you any harm?" "Why, they say it is good on a rainy morning, sir," replied Macdonald. "Oh, yes, famous of a rainy morning, Mr. Sergeant —a mighty *antifogmatic*. It prevents the ague, Mr. Sergeant, and clears the throat of the cob webs, sir."

6. "Your honor's health!" said Macdonald, as he turned off a bumper of the strong cordial.

But scarcely had he smacked his lips, before Dick
paraded Selim, a proud, full-blooded steed, that

stepped as though he disdained the earth he
walked upon.

7. Here the old fellow broke out again: "There,
Mr. Sergeant, there is a horse for you! A charger
fit for a king. Well, my compliments to Colonel
Tarleton. Tell him I have sent him my young
Selim—my Grand Turk. Say to him that he is
too noble for me, and that the only work fit for
him is to drive the rebels out of the country."
And, to send Selim off in high style, he ordered

Dick to bring down his new saddle and holsters, with his silver-mounted pistols. Then, giving Macdonald a hot breakfast, and lending him a great-coat, as it was raining, he let him go.

8. The next morning he waited upon Colonel Tarleton, and told his name, with the smiling countenance of one who expected to be eaten up with fondness. But Tarleton treated him as an entire stranger. After recovering a little, he bluntly asked Colonel Tarleton how he liked his charger. "Charger, sir!" replied Tarleton. "Yes, sir, the elegant horse I sent you yesterday by your sergeant." "An elegant horse by my sergeant? I really don't understand this!"

9. The looks and voice of Colonel Tarleton too sadly convinced the old traitor that he had been bit, and that young Selim was gone. To have been outwitted in this manner by a rebel—to have lost his peach-brandy, his hot breakfast, his great-coat, his new saddle, his silver-mounted pistols, and, worse than all, his darling horse, his young, full-blooded, bounding Selim — the sense of all these losses came crowding upon him so suddenly that the old sinner liked to have suffocated on the spot. He grew black in the face, and as soon as he could recover breath he broke out into a tor-

rent of curses against the rebels generally, and Macdonald in particular.

10. And Selim! a noble horse he was indeed! Full sixteen hands high, with the eye of a hawk, the spirit of a king-eagle, the chest of a lion, swifter than a roebuck, and strong as a buffalo! Macdonald kept Selim up lustily to the top of his mettle. The horse soon learned his master's ways, and at the first glimpse of the red-coats he would paw and champ his bit with rage; and the moment he heard the word " Go!" off he was among them like a thunderbolt.

XXVI.—GENERAL SCHUYLER.

1. In the year 1781 the war was chiefly carried on in the South, but the North was constantly troubled by parties of Tories and Indians, who would swoop down on some small settlements, and make off with whatever they could lay their hands on.

2. During this time General Schuyler was staying at his house, which stood just outside the stockade or walls of Albany. The British com-

mander sent out a party of Tories and Indians to
capture General Schuyler.

3. When they reached the outskirts of the city,
they learned from a Dutch laborer, whom they
had taken, that the general's house was guarded
by six soldiers, three watching by night, and three
by day. They then let the Dutchman go, after
making him swear an oath of secrecy. This oath
he did not keep very strictly, for, the minute the
band was out of sight, he took to his short legs
·and warned the general of their approach.

4. On one of those scorching August days,
when you feel as if you hardly had energy enough
to move, and when the very trees droop their dusty
leaves, too lazy to hold up their heads, Schuyler
and his family were sitting in the large hall, when
a servant entered and told the general that there
was a strange man at the back door who wished
to see him.

5. Schuyler, understanding the trap, gathered
his family in one of the upper rooms, and, giving
orders that the doors and windows should be
barred, fired a pistol from one of the top-story
windows to alarm the neighborhood. The guards,
who had been lounging in the shade of a tree,
started to their feet at the sound of the pistol;

but, alas! too late, for they found themselves surrounded by a crowd of dusky figures, who bound
them hand and foot, before they had time to resist.

6. In the room up-stairs was the sturdy general, standing resolutely by the door, with his gun
in hand, his black slaves gathered around him,
each with some weapon. At the other end of the
room the women were huddled together, some
weeping, some praying. Suddenly, a crash is
heard, which chills the very blood, and brings
vividly to each one's mind the tales of Indian
massacres so common at that day. The band had
broken in at one of the windows.

7. At that moment, Mrs. Schuyler springing to
her feet, rushed to the door; for she remembered
that the baby, only a few months old, having been
forgotten in the hour of flight, was asleep in its
cradle on the first floor. But the general, catching her in his arms, told her that her life was of
more value than her child's, and that, if any one
must go, he would. While, however, this gener-
ous struggle was going on, the third daughter,
gliding past them, was soon at the side of the
cradle. All was as black as night in the hall,
save for a small patch of light just at the foot of

the stairs; this came from the dining-room, where
the Indians could be seen pillaging the shelves,
pulling down the china, and quarreling with one
another over their ill-gotten booty.

8. How to get past the spot was the question,
but the girl did not hesitate. She reached the
cradle unobserved, and was just darting back with
her precious burden, when, by ill-luck, one of the
savages happened to see her. Whiz! went his
sharp tomahawk, within a few inches of the baby's
head, and, clearing the edge of the brave girl's
dress, stuck deep in the stair-rail.

9. Just then one of the Tories, seeing her flit
by, and supposing her to be a servant, called after
her, "Wench, wench, where is your master?" She,
stopping a moment, called back, "Gone to alarm
the town!" and, hurrying on, was soon again with
her father up-stairs.

10. And now, nearly all the plunder having
been secured, the band was about to proceed to
the real object of the expedition, when the general,
raising one of the windows, called out in lusty
tones, as if commanding a large body of men:
"Come on, my brave fellows! Surround the house!
Secure the villains who are plundering!" The
cowards knew that voice, and they each and every

one of them took to the woods as fast as their legs would carry them, leaving the general in possession of the field.

XXVII.—ODE.

1. How sleep the brave who sink to rest,
   With all their country's wishes blest!
   When Spring, with dewy fingers cold,
   Returns to deck their hallowed mold.
   She then shall dress a sweeter sod
   Than Fancy's feet have ever trod.

2. By fairy-hands their knell is rung;
   By forms unseen their dirge is sung;
   Then Honor comes, a pilgrim gray,
   To bless the turf that wraps their clay;
   And Freedom shall awhile repair,
   And dwell a weeping hermit there.
   —*Collins.*

SCOTTISH STORIES.

XXVIII.—EDINBURGH CASTLE.

1. WHILE Robert Bruce was gradually getting possession of the country, and driving out the English, Edinburgh, the principal town of Scotland, remained with its strong castle in possession of the invaders. Sir Thomas Randolph was extremely desirous to gain this important place, but the castle is situated on a very steep and lofty rock, so that it is difficult, or almost impossible even, to get up to the foot of the walls, much more to climb over them. So, while Randolph was considering what was to be done, there came to him a Scottish gentleman, named Francis, who had joined Bruce's standard, and asked to speak with him in private. He then told Randolph that in his youth he had lived in the castle of Edinburgh, and that his father had then been governor of the fortress.

2. It happened at that time that Francis was much in love with a lady who lived in a part of the town beneath the castle, which is called the Grass-Market. Now, as he could not get out of the castle by day to see his mistress, he had prac ticed a way of clambering by night down the castle crag on the steep side, and returning up at his pleasure; when he came to the foot of the wall he made use of a ladder to get over it, as it was not very high on that point, those who built it having trusted to the steepness of the crag. Fran· cis had gone and come so frequently in this dan· gerous manner that, though it was now long ago, he told Randolph he knew the road so well that he would undertake to guide a small party of men by night to the bottom of the wall, and, as they might bring ladders with them, there would be no difficulty in scaling it. The great risk was that of their being discovered by the watchmen while in the act of ascending the cliff, in which case every man of them must perish.

3. Nevertheless, Randolph did not hesitate to attempt the adventure. He took with him only thirty men, and came one dark night to the foot of the crag, which they began to ascend under the guidance of Francis, who went before them, upon

his hands and feet, where there was scarce room to support themselves. All the while these thirty men were obliged to follow in a line, one after the other, by a path that was fitter for a cat than for a man. The noise of a stone falling, or a word spoken from one to another, would have alarmed the watchmen. They were obliged, therefore, to move with the greatest precaution. When they were far up the crag, and near the foundation of the wall, they heard the guards going their rounds, to see that all was safe in and about the castle.

4. Randolph and his party had nothing for it but to lie close and quiet, each man under the crag, as he happened to be placed, and trust that the guards would pass by without noticing them. And while they were waiting in breathless alarm, they got a new cause of fright. One of the soldiers of the castle, willing to startle his comrades, suddenly threw a stone from the wall, and cried out, "Aha! I see you well!" The stone came thundering down over the heads of Randolph and his men, who naturally thought themselves discovered. If they had stirred, or made the slightest noise, they would have been destroyed, for the soldiers above might have killed every man of

7

them, merely by rolling down stones. But being courageous and chosen men, they remained quiet, and the English soldiers, who thought their comrade was merely playing them a trick (as indeed he was), passed on, without further examination.

5. Then Randolph and his men got up and came in haste to the foot of the wall, which was not above twice a man's height in that place. They planted the ladders they had brought, and Francis mounted first to show them the way; Sir Andrew Grey, a brave knight, followed him; and Randolph himself was the third man who got over. Then the rest followed. When once they were within the walls, there was not so much to do, for the garrison were asleep, and unarmed, excepting the watch, who were speedily destroyed. Thus was Edinburgh Castle taken, in the year 1312–'13.

XXIX.—SCOTTISH STRATEGY.

1. THERE was a strong castle near Linlithgow, where an English governor, with a powerful garrison, lay in readiness to support the English cause, and used to exercise much severity upon the

Scotch in the neighborhood. There lived, at no great distance from this stronghold, a farmer, a bold and stout man, whose name was Binnock, or, as it is now pronounced, Binning. This man saw with great joy the progress which the Scotch were making in recovering their country from the English, and resolved to do something to help his countrymen, by getting possession, if it were possible, of the Castle of Linlithgow. But the place was very strong, situated by the side of a lake, defended not only by gates, which were usually kept shut against strangers, but also by a portcullis. A portcullis is a sort of door formed of cross-bars of iron, like a gate. It has not hinges like a door, but is drawn up by pulleys, and let down when any danger approaches. It may be let go in a moment, and then falls down into the doorway, and, as it has great iron spikes at the bottom, it crushes all that it lights upon; and in case of a sudden alarm, a portcullis may be let suddenly fall, to defend the entrance when it is not possible to shut the gates. Binnock knew this very well, but he resolved to be provided against this risk also when he attempted to surprise the castle.

2. So he spoke with some bold, courageous

countrymen, and engaged them in the enterprise, which he accomplished thus: Binnock had been accustomed to supply the garrison of Linlithgow with hay, and he had been ordered by the English governor to furnish some cart-loads, of which they were in want. He promised to bring it accordingly; but, in the night before he drove the hay to the castle, he stationed a party of his friends, as well armed as possible, near the entrance, where they could not be seen by the garrison, and gave them directions that they should come to his assistance as soon as they should hear him give a signal, which was to be, " Call all, call all ! " Then he loaded his cart, and placed eight strong men, well armed, lying flat on their breasts, and covered over with hay, so that they could not be seen. He himself walked carelessly beside the wagon; and he chose the stoutest and bravest of his servants to be the driver, who carried at his belt a stout axe or hatchet.

3. In this way Binnock approached the castle early in the morning; and the watchman, who only saw two men, Binnock being one of them, with a cart of hay, which they expected, opened the gates, and raised up the portcullis to permit them to enter the castle. But as soon as the cart

had got under the gateway, Binnock made a sign to his servant, who with his axe suddenly cut asunder the soam (that is, the yoke which fastens the horses to the cart), and the horses, finding themselves free, naturally started forward, the cart remaining behind. At the same moment Binnock cried, as loud as he could, " Call all, call all !" and drawing his sword, which he had under his country habit, he killed the porter. The armed men then jumped up from under the hay, where they lay concealed, and rushed on the English guard. The Englishmen tried to shut the gates, but they could not, because the cart of hay remained in the gateway, and prevented the folding-doors from being closed. The portcullis was also let fall, but the grating was caught on the cart, and so could not drop to the ground. The men who were in ambush near the gate, hearing the cry, " Call all, call all !" ran to assist those who had leaped out from among the hay ; the castle was taken, and all the Englishmen killed or made prisoners. King Robert rewarded Binnock by bestowing on him an estate, which his posterity afterward enjoyed.

XXX.—CASTLE DANGEROUS.

1. Roxburgh was then a very large castle, situated near where two fine rivers, the Tweed and the Teviot, join each other. Being within five or six miles of the border, the English were extremely desirous of retaining it, and the Scots equally so of obtaining possession of it.

2. It was upon the night of what is called Shrove-tide, a holiday, which Roman Catholics paid great respect to, and solemnized, with much gayety and feasting.

3. Most of the garrison of Roxburgh Castle were feasting and drinking, but still they had set watches on the battlements of the castle, in case of any sudden attack; for, as the Scots had succeeded in so many enterprises of the kind, and as Douglas was known to be in the neighborhood, they thought themselves obliged to keep a very strict guard.

4. There was also an Englishwoman, the wife of one of the officers, who was sitting on the battlements with her child in her arms, and, looking out on the fields below, she saw some black objects, like a herd of cattle, straggling in near the foot of the wall, and approaching the ditch or

moat of the castle. She pointed them out to the sentinel, and asked him what they were. "Pooh, pooh!" said the soldier, "it is Farmer Such-a-man's cattle" (naming a man whose farm lay near to the castle). "The good man is keeping a jolly Shrove-tide, and has forgot to shut up his bullocks in their yard; but if the Douglas come across them before morning, he is likely to rue his negligence."

5. Now, these creeping objects they saw from the castle were no real cattle, but Douglas himself and his soldiers, who had put black cloaks above their armor, and were creeping about on their hands and feet, in order, without being observed, to get so near to the foot of the castle-wall as to be able to set ladders to it. The poor woman, who knew nothing of this, sat quietly on the wall, and began to sing to her child. You must know that the name of Douglas was become so terrible to the English, that the women used to frighten their children with it, and say to them, when they behaved ill, that they would make the Black Douglas take them. And this soldier's wife was singing to her child:

"Hush ye, hush ye, little pet ye;
Hush ye, hush ye, do not fret ye;
The Black Douglas shall not get thee."

"You are not so sure of that!" said a voice close beside her. She felt at that moment a heavy hand, with an iron glove, laid on her shoulder, and when she looked round, she saw the very Black Douglas, she had been singing about, standing close beside her, a tall, swarthy, strong man. At the same time another Scotsman was seen ascending the walls near to the sentinel. The soldier gave the alarm, and rushed at the Scotsman, whose name was Simon Ledehouse, with his lance; but Simon parried the blow, and, closing with the sentinel, struck him a deadly blow with his dagger.

6. The rest of the Scots followed to assist Douglas and Ledehouse, and the castle was taken. Many of the soldiers were put to death, but Douglas protected the woman and the child. I dare say she made no more songs about the Black Douglas.

XXXI.—THE BLACK AGNES.

1. AMONG the warlike exploits of this period, we must not forget the defense of the Castle of Dunbar, by the celebrated Countess of March. Her lord had embraced the side of David Bruce,

and had taken the field with the regent. The countess, who from her complexion was termed Black Agnes, by which name she is still familiarly remembered, was a high-spirited and courageous woman, the daughter of Thomas Randolph, Earl of Moray, and the heiress of his valor and patriotism. The Castle of Dunbar itself was very strong, being built upon a chain of rocks stretching into the sea, having only one passage to the mainland, which was well fortified. It was besieged by Montague, Earl of Salisbury, who employed to destroy its walls great military engines, constructed to throw huge stones, with which machines fortifications were attacked before the use of cannon.

2. Black Agnes set all his attempts at defiance, and showed herself with her maids on the walls of, the castle, wiping the places where the huge stones fell with a clean towel, as if they could do no ill to her castle, save raising a little dust, which a napkin could wipe away. The Earl of Salisbury then commanded them to bring forward to the assault an engine of another kind, being a species of wooden shed, or house, rolled forward on wheels, with a roof of peculiar strength, which, from resembling the ridge of a hog's back, occa

sioned the machine to be called a sow. This, ac-cording to the old mode of warfare, was thrust up to the walls of a besieged castle or city, and served to protect from the arrows and stones of the be-sieged a party of soldiers placed within the sow, who were in the mean while to undermine the wall, or break an entrance through it with pick-axes and mining-tools. When the Countess of March saw this engine advanced to the walls of the castle, she called out to the Earl of Salisbury in derision, and making a kind of rhyme—

"Beware, Montagow,
For farrow shall thy sow!"

At the same time she made a signal, and a huge fragment of rock, which hung prepared for the purpose, was dropped down from the wall upon the sow, whose roof was thus dashed to pieces. As the English soldiers who had been within it were running away as fast as they could to get out of the way of the arrows and stones from the wall, Black Agnes called out, "Behold the litters of English pigs!"

3. The Earl of Salisbury could jest also on such serious occasions. One day he rode near the walls with a knight dressed in armor of proof having three folds of mail over an acton, or leath-

ern jacket: notwithstanding which, one William
Spens shot an arrow with such force that it penetrated all these defenses and reached the heart
of the wearer. "That is one of my lady's love-
tokens," said the earl, as he saw the knight fall
dead from his horse. "Black Agnes's love-shafts
pierce to the heart!"

4. Upon another occasion, the Countess of
March had well-nigh made the Earl of Salisbury
her prisoner. She made one of her people enter
into a treaty with the besiegers, pretending to
betray the castle. Trusting to this agreement, the
earl came at midnight before the gate, which he
found open, and the portcullis drawn up. As Salisbury was about to enter, one John Copland, a
squire of Northumberland, pressed on before him,
and, as soon as he passed the threshold, the portcullis was dropped; and thus the Scots missed
their principal prey, and made prisoner only a
person of inferior condition.

5. At length, the Castle of Dunbar was re-
lieved by Alexander Ramsay, of Dalwolsy, who
brought the countess supplies by sea, both of men
and provisions. The Earl of Salisbury, learning
this, despaired of success, and raised the siege,
which had lasted nineteen weeks. The minstrels

made songs in praise of the perseverance and courage of Black Agnes.   The following lines are nearly the sense of what is preserved :

6. "She kept a stir in tower and trench,
The brawling, boisterous Scottish wench ;
Came I early, came I late,
I found Agnes at the gate."

XXXII.—A LITTLE MAID.

1. Away off in the beautiful country of Greece, a long, long time ago, there lived a little maiden, the daughter of a king. Her name was Gorgo—not a very pretty name, perhaps, to us who are used to calling little girls Maud and Ethel and Helen, but a strong name, and therefore quite appropriate to the little maid who bore it, as you shall see. In those old times there used to be many wars, and the country of Sparta, the part of Greece where Gorgo lived, was famous for its brave warriors, who never thought for a moment of their own safety when their country was in danger. Sometimes these were not good wars, but wars for spite and revenge, instead of for freedom and for loyalty to beautiful Greece.

2. Some wicked man would wish to avenge an injury he had received, and in order to do this

he would go about among the different kingdoms and persuade the rulers to join with him and try to overcome his enemy; and then there would be terrible bloodshed in order to satisfy one wicked man's revenge. Aristagoras was such a man as this. He was dissatisfied with his king, and wished to become a king himself instead. One day he came to Sparta on this evil errand, and tried to persuade King Cleomenes, the father of little Gorgo, to help his base project. He talked with the king a long time. He promised him power and honor and money if he would do as he wished; more and more money, and, as the king refused, still more and more money he offered, and at last the king almost consented.

3. But it had happened that when Aristagoras had come into the presence of the king, the king's little daughter was standing by his side with her hand in his. Aristagoras wanted Cleomenes to send her away, for he knew very well that it is much harder to induce a man to do something wrong when there is a dear little child at his side. But the king had said, "No, say what you have to say in her presence, too." And so little Gorgo had sat at her father's feet, looking up into his face with her innocent eyes, and listening intently

to all that was said. She felt that something was wrong, and when she saw her father look troubled and hesitate, and cast down his eyes, she knew the strange visitor was trying to make him do something he did not quite want to do. She stole her little hand softly into her father's, and said, "Papa, come away—come, or this strange man will make you do wrong."

4. This made the king feel strong again, and, clasping the little maid's hand tightly in his own, he rose and left the tempter, and went away with the child who had saved him and his country from dishonor. Gorgo was only ten years old then, but she was worthy to be a king's daughter, because, being good and true herself, she helped her father to be good and true also.

5. When she grew to be a woman she became the wife of a king, and then she showed herself as noble a queen as she had been a princess. Her husband was that King Leonidas who stood in the narrow pass of Thermopylæ with his small army, and fought back the great hosts of the Persians until he and all his heroic band were killed. But, before this happened, there was a time when the Grecians did not know that the great Persian army was coming to try and destroy

them, and a friend of theirs, who was a prisoner in the country where the great Xerxes lived, wishing to warn the Spartans of the coming of the Persians, so that they might prepare, sent a messenger to King Leonidas. But when the messenger arrived, all he had to show for his message was a bare, white waxen tablet. The king and all the lords puzzled over this strange tablet a long time, but could make nothing out of it. At last they began to think it was done for a jest, and did not mean anything.

6. But just then the young Queen Gorgo said, "Let me take it," and after looking it all over she exclaimed, "There must be some writing underneath the wax!" They scraped away the wax from the tablet, and there, sure enough, written on the wood beneath, was the message of the Grecian prisoner and his warning to King Leonidas.

7. Thus Gorgo helped her country a second time; for, if the Spartans had not known that the army was coming, they could not have warned the other kingdoms, and perhaps the Persians would not have been conquered. But as it was, Leonidas and the other kings called their armies together, and, when the Persian host came sweeping over the plains, the Greeks were ready to

8

meet them, and to fight and die for their beautiful Greece.

8. So this one little maid of hundreds of years ago, princess and queen, helped to save her father from disgrace and her country from ruin. And we may feel sure that she was strong and true to the last, even when her brave husband, Leonidas, lay dead in the fearful pass of Thermopylæ, and she was left to mourn in the royal palace at Sparta.

XXXIII.—ALEXANDER SELKIRK.

1. NEARLY two hundred years ago, an Englishman, living in London, named Daniel Defoe, wrote the story of Robinson Crusoe to interest and amuse boys and girls. Only think of it! Before that time nobody knew anything about the lonely island, or about the ship that was wrecked there. Nobody could know that Robinson was washed ashore and saved. Nobody could see him build his hut, and plan how to live day by day. Nobody could see his tame goats run out to meet him, or hear his parrot cry, " Poor Robinson Crusoe!" Nobody could form the acquaintance of

the faithful man Friday, whom Robinson saved from the cannibals, and who became such a dear friend to him. None of this could any boy or girl at that time enjoy, because the story had not yet come out of the head of Defoe.

2. But, while Robinson Crusoe is a story that never really happened, Daniel Defoe had something to make it out of. In 1704 a Scotch sailor, named Alexander Selkirk, then twenty-eight years old, was left upon Juan Fernandez, an uninhabited island in the Pacific, off the coast of Chili. He had quarreled with the captain of the ship in which he sailed, and the captain sent him ashore to improve his temper. Here he lived alone for four years and four months, when, an English vessel appearing, he was carried back to his native country.

3. About half of what is said to have happened to Robinson Crusoe really happened to Alexander Selkirk. The hut was built; search was made for food; fish were drawn from the water, and turtles found upon the shore. Cabbage-palm grew in the woods, and, from seeds found in the wrecked vessels, turnips, parsnips, and radishes were grown. The goats, too, were a living reality, and, when his powder gave out, the active

young Scotchman could run down a young goat, and so secure a dinner.

4. Here this sailor remained during the long years, busy and lonesome. The poet Cowper has supposed that he was made entirely unhappy by his longing for society and friends, and has expressed his supposed sentiments in the following poem: ·

5. I am monarch of all I survey;
My right there is none to dispute:
From the center all round to the sea,
I am lord of the fowl and the brute.

O Solitude! where are the charms
That sages have seen in thy face?
Better dwell in the midst of alarms,
Than reign in this horrible place.

6. I am out of humanity's reach;
I must finish my journey alone;
Never hear the sweet music of speech;
I start at the sound of my own.
The beasts that roam over the plain
My form with indifference see;
They are so unacquainted with man,
Their tameness is shocking to me.

7. Society, friendship, and love,
Divinely bestowed upon man,
Oh, had I the wings of a dove,
How soon would I taste you again!
My sorrows I then might assuage
In the ways of religion and truth;
Might learn from the wisdom of age,
And be cheered by the sallies of youth.

8. Religion! what treasures untold
Reside in that heavenly word!
More precious than silver and gold,
Or all that the earth can afford.

But the sound of the church-going bell
  These valleys and rocks never heard,
Never sighed at the sound of a knell,
  Or smiled when the Sabbath appeared.

9. But the sea-fowl has gone to her nest,
  The beast has laid down in his lair;
Even here is a season of rest,
  And I to my cabin repair.
There's mercy in every place;
  And mercy, encouraging thought,
Gives even affliction a grace,
  And reconciles man to his lot.

10. Selkirk might sometimes have indulged in thoughts like these, but generally he was too busy to give much heed to them. Besides, the life itself had its charms, and, after his rough usage upon the ship, he keenly felt the joy of perfect freedom. Then the animals which he tamed began to appear as real friends, and, though no man Friday came to cheer and comfort him, he began to really love his new home and enjoy the life which he led.

11. This is the account given of the appear-ance of Selkirk by Rogers, captain of the vessel that finally took Selkirk off from the island : " At night, after we came to anchor, we discovered a

bright light upon the island. In the morning we sent our yawl ashore with six men, all armed, and, as it was gone some time, we sent our pinnace, with the men armed, for we were afraid lest the Spaniards were there and had seized our boat. We put out a signal for the boat, when our pin- nace returned from the shore and brought abun- dance of craw-fish, with a man clothed in goat- skins, who looked wilder than the first owners of them. At his first coming on board us, he had so much forgot his language for want of use that one could scarcely understand him, for he seemed to speak his words by halves. We offered him a dram, but he would not touch it, having drunk nothing but water since he came upon the island, and it was some time before he could relish our victuals.

12. " He took goats by speed of foot, for his way of living, and continual exercise of walking and running, cleared him of all gross humors, so that he ran with wonderful swiftness through the woods, and up the rocks and hills. We had a bull-dog, which we sent with several of our nim- blest runners, to help him in catching goats, but he tired both the dog and men, caught the goats, and brought them back to us. Being forced to shift

without shoes, his feet had become so hard that he ran everywhere without annoyance; and it was some time before he could wear shoes after we found him; for, not being used to any so long, his feet swelled when he came first to use them again."

13. Selkirk returned to his native country, married, and settled down to a steady life. He never forgot his lonely isle, and often wished himself back among his goats and cats. He learned dram-drinking once more, and, as he began to eat and drink as people did around him, he lost much of the health and strength which he gained in his solitary home. From him we may all learn that the simple, natural way of living may be the best for us in giving us health to enjoy life and perform our duties.

XXXIV.—THE OLD-FASHIONED SCHOOL.

1. IMAGINE yourselves in Master Ezekiel Cheever's school-room. It is a large, dingy room, with a sanded floor, and is lighted by windows that turn on hinges, and have little, diamond-shaped panes of glass. The scholars sit on long benches,

with desks before them. At one end of the room is a great fireplace, so spacious that there is room enough for three or four boys to stand in each of the chimney-corners. This was the good old fashion of fireplaces when there was wood enough in the forests to keep people warm without their digging into the bowels of the earth for coal.

2. It is a winter's day when we take our peep into the school-room. See what logs of wood have been rolled into the fireplace, and what a broad, bright blaze goes leaping up the chimney! And every few moments a vast cloud of smoke is puffed into the room, which sails slowly over the heads of the scholars, until it gradually settles upon the walls and ceiling. They are blackened with the smoke of many years already.

3. Do you see the venerable schoolmaster, severe in aspect, with a black skull-cap on his head, like an ancient Puritan, and the snow of his white beard drifting down to his very girdle? What boy would dare to play or whisper, or even glance aside from his book, while Master Cheever is on the outlook behind his spectacles? For such offenders, if any such there be, a rod of birch is hanging over the fireplace, and a heavy ferule lies on the master's desk.

4. And now school is begun. What a murmur
of multitudinous tongues, like the whispering of

leaves of a wind-stirred oak, as the scholars con
over their various tasks! Buzz! buzz! buzz!
Amid just such a murmur has Master Cheever
spent about sixty years; and long habit has made
it as pleasant to him as the hum of a bee-hive
when the insects are busy in the sunshine. Now

a class in Latin is called to recite. Forth steps a row of queer-looking little fellows, wearing square-skirted coats and small-clothes, with buttons at the knee. They look like so many grandfathers in their second childhood.

5. These lads are to be sent to Cambridge and educated for the learned professions. Old Master Cheever has lived so long, and seen so many generations of school-boys grow up to be men, that now he can almost prophesy what sort of a man each boy will be. One urchin shall hereafter be a doctor, and administer pills and potions, and stalk gravely through life, perfumed with asafœtida. Another shall wrangle at the bar, and fight his way to wealth and honors, and, in his declining age, shall be a worshipful member of his Majesty's Council. A third shall be a worthy successor to the old Puritan ministers now in their graves. But as they are merely school-boys now, their business is to construe Virgil.

6. Next comes a class in arithmetic. These boys are to be the merchants, shopkeepers, and mechanics of a future period. Hitherto they have traded only in marbles and apples. Others will upheave the blacksmith's hammer, or drive the plane over the carpenter's bench, or take the lap-

stone and the awl, and learn the trade of shoe
making. Many will follow the sea, and become
bold, rough sea-captains. Wherefore, teach them
their multiplication-table, good Master Cheever,
and whip them well when they deserve it; for
much of the country's welfare depends on these
boys.

7. But, alas! Master Cheever's watchful eye
has caught two boys at play. Now we shall see
awful times. The malefactors are summoned before the master's chair. Master Cheever has taken
down that terrible birch-rod! Short is the trial—
the sentence quickly passed—and now the judge
prepares to execute it in person. Thwack!
thwack! thwack! In those good old times a
schoolmaster's blows were well laid on. And thus
the forenoon passes away. Now it is twelve
o'clock. The master looks at his great silver
watch, and then, with tiresome deliberation, puts
the ferule into the desk. "You are dismissed,"
says Master Cheever.

8. The boys retire, treading softly until they
have passed the threshold; but fairly out of the
school-room lo, what a joyous shout! What a
scampering and trampling of feet! What care
they for the ferule and birch-rod now? Were boys

created merely to study Latin and arithmetic? No; the better purposes of their being are to sport, to leap, to run, to shout, to slide upon the ice, to snow-ball. Happy boys! Enjoy your play-time now, and come again to study and to feel the birch-rod and the ferule to-morrow.

9. Now the master has set everything to rights, and is ready to go home to dinner. Yet he goes reluctantly. The old man has spent so much of his life in the smoky, noisy, buzzing school-room, that, when he has a holiday, he feels as if his place were lost, and himself a stranger in the world. *Hawthorne.*

XXXV.—STORY OF FRANKLIN'S KITE.

1. It was in the spring of 1752 that Franklin thought of trying the experiment with a kite; and it was during one of the June thunder-storms of that year that the immortal kite was flown.

2. Who does not know the story? How he made his kite of a large silk handkerchief, and fastened to the top of the perpendicular stick a piece of sharpened iron wire. How he stole away, upon the approach of a storm, into the common not

far from his own house, say about the corner of Race and Eighth Streets, near a spot where there was an old cow-shed. How, wishing to avoid the ridicule of possible failure, he told no one what he was going to do, except his son, who accompanied him, and who was then not the small boy he is represented in a hundred pictures, but a braw lad of twenty-two, one of the beaux of Philadelphia.

3. How the kite was raised in time for the coming gust, the string being hempen, except the part held in the hand, which was silk. How, at the termination of the hempen string, a common key was fastened; and in the shed was deposited a Leyden bottle, in which to collect from the clouds, if the clouds should contain it, the material requisite for an electric shock. How father and son stood for some time under the shed, presenting the spectacle, if there had been any one to behold it, of two escaped lunatics, flying a kite in the rain ; the young gentleman, no doubt, feeling a little foolish. How, at last, when a thundercloud appeared to pass directly over the kite, and yet no sign of electricity appeared, the hopes of the father, too, began to grow faint. How, when both were ready to despair of success, Franklin's heart stood still as he suddenly observed the fibers

of the hempen string to rise, as a boy's hair rises when he stands on the insulating-stool. How, with eager, trembling hand, he applied his knuckle to the key, and drew therefrom an unmistakable spark, and another and another, and as many as he chose. How the Leyden vial was charged, and both received the most thrilling shock ever experienced by man; a shock that might have been figuratively styled electric, if electric it had not really been. How, the wet kite being drawn in, and the apparatus packed, the philosopher went home exulting, the happiest philosopher in Christendom.

4. And this was only the beginning of triumph. The next ships that arrived from the Old World brought him the news that the same experiment, in the mode originally suggested by him, of erecting an iron rod upon an eminence, had been successfully performed in France, so that his name had suddenly become one of the most famous in Europe.

XXXVI.—THE CASE OF JOHN HOOK.

1. Wirt, in his life of Patrick Henry, gives this specimen of the eloquence of the great orator. In Campbell County, Virginia, lived a Scotchman, named Hook, who was suspected of being a Tory. The American army was greatly distressed for food, and a commissary, named Venable, took two of Hook's steers, without his consent, to feed the starving soldiers. After the war, a lawyer, named Cowan, advised Hook to sue Venable for tres- pass. Venable employed Patrick Henry. The case was tried in the old court-house in New Lon- don.

2. Mr. Henry depicted the distress of the American army in the most gloomy colors, and then asked: " Where was the man with an Ameri- can heart, who would not have thrown open his fields, his barns, his cellars, the doors of his house, the portals of his breast, to have received with open arms the meanest soldier of that little band of famished patriots? Where is the man? There he stands; but whether the heart of an American beats in his bosom, you, gentlemen, are to judge?" He then carried the jury, by the powers of his imagination, to the plains around York, the sur-

render of which had followed shortly after the act complained of.

3. He depicted the surrender in the most glowing and noble colors of his eloquence. The audience saw before their eyes the dejection of the British as they marched out of the trenches; they saw the triumph which lighted up every patriotic face, and heard the shouts of victory and the cry of "Washington and liberty!" as it rang through the American ranks and echoed back from hill and shore. "But hark! what notes of discord are these which disturb the general joy? They are notes of John Hook, hoarsely bawling through the American camp, '*Beef! beef! beef!*'"

4. The whole audience was convulsed. The clerk of the court, unable to contain himself, and unwilling to disturb the court, rushed out of the court-house and threw himself on the grass in the most violent paroxysm of laughter, where he was rolling when Hook, with very different feelings, came out into the yard for relief also. "Jemmy Steptoe," he said to the clerk, "what ails ye, mon?" Mr. Steptoe was only able to say that he could not help it. "Never mind ye," said Hook; "wait till Billy Cowan gets up; he'll show him the la'!" But Mr. Cowan could scarcely utter a word. The

9

jury instantly returned a verdict against Hook.
The people were highly excited, and Hook was
obliged to leave the county to avoid a coat of tar
and feathers.

XXXVII.—THE FIRST STEAMBOAT IN THE WEST.

1. MANY things combined to make the year
1811 the wonderful year of the West. During
the earlier months, the waters of many of the great
rivers overflowed their banks, so that the whole
country was covered from bluff to bluff. Widespread sickness followed, such as had never before
been known. A spirit of change and uneasiness
seemed to seize the very inhabitants of the forest.
A countless multitude of squirrels, obeying some
great and universal impulse, left their joyous,
gamboling life and their ancient retreats in the
North, and were seen pressing forward by tens
of thousands in a deep and sober phalanx to the
South. No obstacles seemed to check this extraordinary and united movement. The word had
been given them to go forth, and they obeyed it,

though multitudes perished in the broad Ohio, which lay in their path.

2. The splendid comet of that year long con-tinued to shed its twilight over the forests. As the autumn drew to a close, the whole Mississippi Valley, from the Missouri to the Gulf, was shaken to its center by continued earthquakes. It was at this very time, when so many extraordinary events of Nature combined to spread wonder and awe, that the first steamboat was seen descending the great rivers, and the awe-struck Indian on the

banks beheld the Pinelore, or "fire-canoe," flying
through the turbid waters.

3. The banks of the Ohio and its tributaries
were covered with innumerable farms; and rafts,
flat-boats, and barges of every description, laden
with the produce, floated upon its wide surface,
toward the general market of the West, New Orleans. Besides the barges and vessels of heavy
burden, which made their long annual voyage to
and from the city, the river was covered, particularly in time of flood, by thousands of queer machines, for boats they can hardly be called, most
of which soon disappeared. From seventy to
eighty days were consumed in thus effecting the
long and monotonous voyage from Pittsburg to
New Orleans.

4. The experiments in steam navigation made
on the Hudson River and adjoining waters, previous to the year 1809, were attended with complete
success. Attention was now paid to the Western
rivers, and Mr. Roosevelt, of New York, accompanied by Mr. Fulton, visited these rivers to see
whether they would admit of steam navigation.
At this time two boats, the North River and the
Clermont, were running on the Hudson. Mr.
Roosevelt surveyed the rivers from Pittsburg to

New Orleans, and made a favorable report, and it was decided to build a boat at the former town.

5. Accordingly, during the year 1811 the first boat was launched on the waters of the Ohio. It was called the Orleans, and was intended to ply between Natchez, in the State of Mississippi, and the city whose name it bore. In October it left Pittsburg for a trial voyage. No freight or passengers were taken. Mr. Roosevelt with his family; Mr. Baker, the engineer; Andrew Jack, the pilot; and six hands, with a few domestics, formed her whole burden. There were no wood-yards at that time, and constant delays were unavoidable.

6. Late at night on the fourth day after quitting Pittsburg, they arrived safely at Louisville, having been but seventy hours descending upward of seven hundred miles. The novel appearance of the vessel, and the fearful rapidity with which it made its passage over the broad reaches of the river, excited both terror and surprise among many of the settlers along the banks, whom the rumor of such an invention had never reached.

7. The unexpected arrival of the boat at Louisville, in the course of a fine, still, moonlight night, created a great stir. The extraordinary sound which filled the air as the pent-up steam was suf-

fered to escape on rounding-to, produced a general alarm, and multitudes in the town rose from their beds to see what was the matter. It was related that an impression widely prevailed that the comet had fallen into the Ohio.

8. The low stage of water caused a detention at Louisville until the last week in November, when the voyage was resumed. When the boat arrived at a point five miles above the Yellow Banks, she was moored to take in wood. While thus engaged, our voyagers were accosted in great alarm by the squatters of the neighborhood, who inquired if they had heard strange noises on the river and in the woods on the preceding day, or had seen the shores shake.

9. Hitherto nothing extraordinary had been perceived. The following day they pursued their monotonous voyage in those vast solitudes. The air was misty, still, and dull. Though the sun was visible, like a glowing ball of copper, his rays hardly shed more than a mournful twilight on the surface of the water. Evening drew nigh, and with it some indications of what was passing around them became evident. And as they sat on deck, they ever and anon heard a rushing sound and violent splash, and saw large portions of the

shore tearing away from the land and falling into the river.

10. It was, as my informant said, " an awful day, so still that you could have heard a pin drop on the deck. They spoke little, for every one on board appeared thunderstruck. The comet had disappeared about this time, which circumstance was noticed with awe by the crew. The trees were seen waving and nodding on the bank without a wind. Toward evening of the second day they found themselves at a loss for a place of shelter. The pilot said that he was lost; that the channel was everywhere altered. A large island in mid-channel familiar to the pilot was sought in vain, having entirely disappeared.

11. Thus in doubt and terror, they proceeded hour after hour till dark, when they found a small island and rounded-to. Here they lay, keeping watch on deck during the long autumnal night, and listening to the sound of the roaring waters. Several times in the course of the night earthquake-shocks were felt. It was a long night, but morning dawned and showed them that they were near the mouth of the Ohio.

12. About noon that day they reached the small town of New Madrid, on the right bank of

the Mississippi. Here they found the inhabitants in the greatest distress and consternation. Part of the population had fled in terror to the higher grounds; others prayed to be taken on board, as the earth was opening in fissures on every side, and their houses hourly falling around them.

13. At that time you floated for three or four hundred miles on the rivers without seeing a human habitation. Proceeding from New Madrid, after many days of great danger, they reached their destination at Natchez in January, 1812, to the great astonishment of all, the escape of the boat having been considered an impossibility.

XXXVIII.—THE POWER OF KINDNESS.

1. WILLIAM SAVERY was a Quaker, living near Philadelphia, during the Revolutionary War. He was a kindly-disposed man, and many were his charitable deeds that the public knew nothing about. He was a tanner by trade, and one night a number of hides were stolen from his yard. While he suspected a neighbor of his, a worthless sort of fellow, he had no proof against him. He

said nothing about his loss, but the next day the following advertisement appeared in the papers:

2. " Whoever stole a lot of hides on the 5th of the present month, is hereby informed that the owner has a sincere wish to be his friend. If poverty tempted him to this false step, the owner will keep the whole matter secret, and will gladly put him in the way of obtaining a living by means more likely to bring him peace of mind."

3. This odd notice attracted a good deal of attention; but the thief alone knew from whom the kind offer came. When he read it, his heart was filled with sorrow for what he had done. A few nights afterward, as the tanner's family were about going to bed, they heard a timid knock; and, when the door opened, there stood Smith, with the hides on his shoulder. Without looking up, he said : " I have brought these back, Mr. Savery. Where shall I put them ?"

4. " Wait till I can light a lantern, and I will go to the barn with thee," replied Mr. Savery. " Then, perhaps, thou wilt come in and tell me how this thing happened, and we will see what can be done for thee."

5. As soon as they were gone out, his wife prepared some hot coffee, and placed pies and meat

on the table. When they returned from the barn, she said, "Neighbor Smith, I thought some hot supper would do thee good." Smith turned his back toward her, and did not speak. After a moment, he said in a choked voice: "It is the first time I ever stole anything, and I feel very bad about it. I don't know how it is. I am sure I didn't think once that I should ever come to be what I am. But I took to drinking, and then to quarreling. And since I began to go down-hill, everybody gives me a kick. You are the first man, Mr. Savery, that has ever offered me a helping hand. God bless you! I stole the hides from you, meaning to sell them. But I tell you the truth, when I say it is the first time I was ever a thief."

6. "Let it be the last time, my friend," replied William Savery. "The secret shall be between me and thee. Thou art still young. Promise me that thou will not drink any more liquor for a year, and I will employ thee to-morrow at good wages. Perhaps we may find some work for thy family also. The little boy can at least pick up stones. But eat a bit now, and drink some hot coffee, to keep thee from craving anything stronger. Keep up a brave heart for the sake of thy wife

and children. When thou hast need of coffee, tell Mary, and she will always give it to thee."

7. The poor fellow tried hard to eat and drink, but the food seemed to choke him. He could not smother his feelings, and he bowed his head on the table and wept like a child. By-and-by he ate and drank with good heart; and his host parted with him for the night with this kindly word, "Try to do well, John, and thou wilt always find a friend in me."

8. Smith began to work for him the next day, and remained with him many years, a sober, honest, and faithful man. The secret of the theft was kept between them; but, after John's death, William Savery told the story, to show that evil may be overcome with good.

XXXIX.—OLD IRONSIDES.

1. WHEN war was declared between the United States and Great Britain in 1812, the British power was dominant upon the ocean. Since the times of Sir Francis Drake and the Spanish Armada, the British navy had retained the supremacy

then gained. In three hundred years no British fleet had ever surrendered to an enemy. Such continued success made the British arrogant, and they looked down with contempt upon the naval power of any other people. At the beginning of the war, the American navy was small and weak. It consisted of about twenty vessels, the largest of which were frigates.

2. But the few vessels of the American navy were strongly built, and were manned by officers who had gained their fighting experience in the war with the Barbary states. Neither the officers nor men were in any fear of the great power of Britain, and they particularly hated the British for their habit of impressing American seamen. Thus it happened that all the American command-ers had made up their minds to fight whenever the force against them was anywhere nearly equal, and to fight for victory.

3. Among the vessels of our little navy was the frigate Constitution, better known, from the strength of her build, as "Old Ironsides." At the breaking out of the war she was commanded by Captain Isaac Hull, one of our most expe-rienced naval officers. In August, 1812, Hull sailed on a cruise, looking for an enemy, and in a

short time he fell in with the British frigate Guerriere, a vessel about equal in size to the Constitu-

tion. Both parties advanced eagerly to the conflict, but in thirty minutes the Guerriere was re-
duced to a mere wreck, and the British flag was
hauled down.

4. Captain Hull sailed into Boston Harbor,
where the Old Ironsides was repaired and made
ready for sea. Captain Hull generously resigned,

so as to permit others to have a share of glory, and
Captain Bainbridge was appointed to the command of the Constitution.

5. On December 29th, Captain Bainbridge,
while cruising off the coast of Brazil, encountered
the British frigate Java, one of the best-appointed
ships in the British navy. A running battle en-
sued, which lasted four hours, and so well did
Captain Bainbridge manage his ship that he re-
duced the Java to a wreck, while the damage to
the Constitution was so slight that it was ready
for another fight the next day.

6. Peace between the two countries was arranged at Ghent, between commissioners appointed
by both powers, in December, 1814, but the news
was not received in this country for several weeks.
The Constitution, under the command of Captain
Stewart, sailed from Boston on a cruise in December, and, on the 20th of February, 1815, she encountered two British vessels—the Cyane and Le-
vant—the combined force of which was equal to
that of the Constitution, if not greater. The action commenced at six in the evening, and continued for four hours in the moonlight night. At
ten o'clock, both British vessels were prizes to the
Constitution, while she was so little damaged that

complete repairs were made without making a
port.

7. After the war great improvements were made
in ship-building, and soon the old frigate became
too old-fashioned for active service at sea, and for
a time she was employed as a receiving-ship. At
last it was proposed to withdraw her entirely from
service, and break her up. This proposition roused
the indignation of the poet Holmes, then a boy,
and his hot wrath broke up the project and saved
the ship. She is now used as a school-ship for the
training of seamen. Here follows the poem:

8. Ay! tear her tattered ensign down!
    Long has it waved on high;
And many an eye has danced to see
    That banner in the sky.
Beneath it rang the battle-shout,
    And burst the cannon's roar;
The meteor of the ocean-air
    Shall sweep the clouds no more!

9. Her deck, once red with hero's blood,
    Where knelt the vanquished foe,
When winds were hurrying o'er the flood,
    And waves were white below,

No more shall feel the victor's tread
Or know the conquered knee;
The harpies of the shore shall pluck
The eagle of the sea.

10. Oh! better that her shattered hulk
Should sink beneath the wave;
Her home was on the mighty deep,
And there should be her grave.
Nail to the mast her holy flag,
Set every threadbare sail,
And give her to the god of storms,
The lightning and the gale!

XL.—CHICAGO.

1. It is the evening of October 9, 1871. The great city of the West is settling down into the quiet of the night. The Sabbath has ended. The churches have closed, and citizens of all ranks and kinds are peacefully resting in their homes. The guardians of the night are all out, faithful to watch, quick to detect, and prompt to act. Three hundred thousand people throw off the cares of the day, and seek their needed repose. No cause of

alarm, save the wind, which since noon has risen from a gentle breeze to a fierce gale at sunset. Even now it increases, and in the morning papers

View of Chicago from Madison Street Bridge, before the Fire.

we may expect a catalogue of chimneys blown down, and of houses unroofed. Beyond this there is nothing to fear, and all is well.

2. A little way out from what is now the heart of the town was a section covered with piles of lumber and rows of wooden tenements ready for the torch. The lights are flickering through the

10

dark alleys as a poor woman takes a lamp and goes into a hovel to milk the cow. The blustering wind bids her be careful. An uneasy movement of the cow, and the lamp is overturned into the straw and litter of the stable. A flame shoots up, and the milker has scarcely time to reach the door when the whole building is on fire. She, with her children, rush into the street, as the flame comes in through roof, window, and doorway of her dwelling. Then the roar of the windswept flame and the appalling cry of fire!

3. But the city is prepared for these accidents. The fire-bells ring out their alarm. Trained horses take their places by the steam fire-engines, and the heart has scarcely time to beat before they are on a mad gallop down the streets. In a moment a thousand jets of water will subdue the fire, and the city will again sink to quiet rest.

4. But, swift as the firemen speed to the scene, the flame is swifter still. Borne on the wings of the wind, it leaps from street to street. It is no longer a wind but a tempest, and a tempest of flame. The track of the devouring element broadens and dives toward the heart of the city. Men, women, and children rush frantically to get out of the path of destruction. Down go miles of stately

houses and blocks of business. The reservoirs of grain, the vast hotels, and the spires of churches appear for a moment through the glare, then melt away into ashes. The whole world is in flames!

5. While hope remains, men are active; but now they stand in sullen despair. They look on helpless and hopeless through the long hours of the night. The first rays of the morning reveal a scene of widespread and total desolation. The heart of the city has been consumed. Twenty thousand of its inhabitants are homeless.

6. One consoling thought is left. The fire-fiend is at last curbed, hemmed in on the east by the lake, on the north by the river which stretches between it and the homes in which seventy-five thousand people are peacefully asleep, all unaware of the devastation that has been raging so near them. Surely the fiery foe will not reach those homes. The river is their protection. The comforting thought is but momentary. Already a livid cloud is sweeping across the narrow stream. Burning brands and glowing embers are borne on the wings of a fierce tornado straight toward those peaceful homes.

7. The scene that ensues has no parallel in the history of the world. Who shall arouse those

sleepers and warn them of their peril? Who, now, when the flames are already at the doors, shall bear away the sick ones, the aged, the little children, the babes, to safety? Alas! whither shall they be borne? The lake on one side; on the other, a narrow pathway leading toward the country to the north, along which the flames are rushing with mad rapidity. Every other way of escape is cut off.

8. Many plunge breast-deep into the lake, and there during long hours stand many hundreds of people, feeble women, some with babes in their arms, many sick and aged, till the fire subsides and rescue comes. Nearly one hundred thousand souls are fleeing before the merciless flames. During that fearful Monday this great throng continue their flight without food, without water, scorched by the hot blast, their clothes and often their hair on fire; the stronger bearing the weaker in their arms and on their shoulders, they rush on, every moment pursued by the flames. Many sink to the ground to rise no more, how many never will be known.

9. Finally they are in the open country. It is a strange, weird place to pass a night in, a graveyard, but it is a place of safety from the foe that

all day had pursued them. And there, about ten o'clock at night, as they see the last house on the other side of the city limits crumble to ashes, they sink down to their dismal bivouac, many pillowing their heads upon the graves among which they lay.

10. Many were the "heroic deeds" that had been wrought on that fearful day, heroic deeds of husbands and wives in rescuing each other and their children, of children in rescuing parents and brothers and sisters, of many in helping the helpless when sore pressed themselves, and of all in maintaining the brave, heroic fight against such fearful odds.

11. And now opens another chapter of the "story of heroic deeds" in the history of the Chicago fire. It is the story of the heroism of sympathy, of charity, of generosity, of dauntless energy. How shall these thousands of homeless ones, with winter impending, be sheltered? How food gotten to the famished crowd in the graveyard, who have not tasted food since Sunday night?

12. The city stricken is still quick to act. During Monday, while the conflagration is still raging, relief committees are organizing; the houses of those who are left with houses are being opened to

those who have none; the sound of axe and hammer is heard on every side, erecting barracks and
temporary cabins; men and women are gathering
stores of food and clothing; and loaded wagons
are making their way around the burning city to
reach the encampment in the cemetery and on the
open prairie. The telegraph has also been set to
telling to other cities the story of the great ca-
lamity. Before and during the night trains of
cars come from the whole country for many miles
around, loaded with food, clothing, blankets, and
even delicacies for the sick. And so on to
Tuesday morning the half - famished, homeless
multitude once more welcome their morning meal,
and before night the whole vast multitude on the
streets have obtained some kind of shelter.

13. And now the return click is heard at the
telegraph-offices. Cities too distant to send food
send words of cheer and money. As the day wears
on, the wires can scarcely carry all the messages of
sympathy which come pouring in. London, Paris,
Berlin, all the great cities of Europe, vie with each
other in liberality, and send their substantial offer-
ings through the cable under the sea, and, before
the sun sets, messages of organized aid come from
distant Calcutta and Melbourne. The thrill of

human sympathy had encircled the earth. Nor did the supplies fail until the people of the grateful city cried, " Enough ! "

14. In the old Arabian story, the palace of Aladdin is built in a single night by the aid of magic. But now the wonder wrought by the genii is surpassed. From the ashes of that terrible night a new city grows up, marvelous in its freshness, its strength, and its beauty. No need of magic here, or rather the only magic needed is that of self-reliance and the sympathy of the world so bountifully expressed.

15. With a full heart the poet Whittier describes the scene, and the lesson to be derived from it:

> Men said at vespers, " All is well ! "
> In one wild night the city fell;
> Fell shrines of prayer and marts of gain,
> Before the fiery hurricane.

16. On threescore spires had sunset shone,
Where ghastly sunrise looked on none.
Men clasped each other's hands, and said,
" The City of the West is dead ! "

17. Brave hearts who fought in slow retreat,
The fiends of fire from street to street,

Turned powerless to the blinding glare,
The dumb defiance of despair.

18. A sudden impulse thrilled each wire
That signaled round that sea of fire;
Swift words of cheer, warm heart-throbs came,
In tears of pity died the flame.

19. From East, from West, from South, from
    North,
The messages of hope shot forth,
And underneath the severing wave,
The world, full-handed, reached to save.

20. Fair seemed the old; but fairer still
The new, the dreary void shall fill
With dearer homes than those o'erthrown,
For love shall lay each corner-stone.

21. Rise, stricken city! from thee throw
The ashen sackcloth of thy woe,
And build, as to Amphion's strain,
To songs of cheer thy walls again!

22. How shriveled in thy hot distress
The primal sin of selfishness!
How instant rose, to take thy part,
The angel in the human heart!

23. Ah! not in vain the flames that tossed
    Above thy dreadful holocaust;
    The Christ again has preached through thee
    The Gospel of Humanity!

24. Then lift once more thy towers on high,
    And fret with spires the western sky,
    To tell that God is yet with us,
    And love is still miraculous!

THE END.

THE NEW McGUFFEY READERS

THE value of the McGuffey Readers as educational tools arises from their sound pedagogy, their good literature, and their pure morality.

¶ Their success has depended upon these intrinsic qualities joined to a grade of mechanical excellence unsurpassed; and they have always been sold at a price lower than any other standard series on the market. A new series of McGuffey Readers is now issued, having the same educational aim, and offered at even lower prices than the other series. The New McGuffey Readers have had the same editorial control in their preparation that was exercised in the revision of 1878, and although published but a short time, have already received the same cordial reception that was given the former edition.

¶ Teachers who like the McGuffey ideal of a perfect reader—those who wish easy gradation, pure morality, the highest examples of literature adapted not only to thought culture but also to voice culture — will gladly welcome books on this plan that contain new material. On the other hand, teachers whose lives have been partly formed in the mold set by the older McGuffey, will be glad to find their old favorite selections preserved in this latest edition. The plan has been to reject the old, wherever improvement could be made ; but to retain classic selections where change would injure.

¶ The New McGuffey Readers are mechanically the best possible product of the artist, the engraver, the compositor, the printer, and the binder. No expense and no effort have been spared to make the books worthy of issue in this newly begun century, and worthy of use by another generation of pupils.

AMERICAN BOOK COMPANY

MILNE'S PROGRESSIVE ARITHMETICS

By WILLIAM J. MILNE, Ph.D., LL.D., President of New York State Normal College, Albany, N. Y.

THREE BOOK SERIES	TWO BOOK SERIES
First Book $0.35	First Book $0.35
Second Book 40	Complete Book 65
Third Book 45	

IN these series the best modern methods of instruction have been combined with those older features which gave the author's previous arithmetics such marvelous popularity. ¶ Built upon a definite pedagogical plan, these books teach the processes of arithmetic in such a way as to develop the reasoning faculties, and to train the power of rapid, accurate, and skillful manipulation of numbers. The inductive method is applied, leading the pupils to discover truths for themselves ; but it is supplemented by model solutions and careful explanations of each step.

¶ Each new topic is first carefully developed, and then enforced by sufficient practice to fix it thoroughly in the mind. The problems, which have been framed with the greatest care, relate to a wide range of subjects drawn from modern life and industries. Reviews in various forms are a marked feature. Usefulness is the keynote.

¶ In the First and Second Books the amount of work that may be accomplished in a half year is taken as the unit of classification, and the various subjects are treated topically, each being preceded by a brief résumé of the concepts already acquired. In the Third Book the purely topical method is used in order to give the pupil a coherent knowledge of each subject. The Complete Book covers the work usually given to pupils during the last four years of school.

AMERICAN BOOK COMPANY

PUPILS' OUTLINE STUDIES IN UNITED STATES HISTORY

$0.30

By FRANCIS H. WHITE, A.M., Professor of History and Political Science, Kansas State Agricultural College

A BLANK book, which is intended for the pupil's use in connection with any good history of the United States. It presents an original combination of devices conveniently arranged, and affords an unusually clear idea of our country's history in which the chief events are deeply impressed on the learner's mind. The entire development of the United States has been taken up in the most logical manner, and facts of a similar nature have been grouped naturally together.
¶ This material is in the form of outline maps, charts, tables, outlines for essays, book references, etc., with full directions for the pupil, and suggestions to the teacher. Students are required to locate places, trace routes, follow lines of development, make pictures of objects illustrating civilization, write compositions, etc.
¶ The use of this book has demonstrated that the teaching of history need no longer present any difficulties to the teacher. Mere memorizing is discouraged, and the pupil is compelled to observe closely, to select essential facts, to classify his knowledge, to form opinions for himself, and to consult the leading authorities. The interest thus instilled will invariably lead to a sufficient grasp of the subject.
¶ The body of the book is divided into the following general headings: The Indians; Discovery and Exploration; Colonization; The Development of Nationality; Military History; The Progress of Civilization; Political History; and Our Flag and Its Defenders. While none of these periods is treated exhaustively, each is taken up so comprehensively and suggestively that further work can be made easily possible where more time is available.

AMERICAN BOOK COMPANY

SUPPLEMENTARY READING

¶ This grading, which is simply suggestive, represents the earliest years in which these books can be read to advantage.

GEOGRAPHY

NATURE STUDY

AMERICAN BOOK COMPANY

SUPPLEMENTARY READING

HISTORY AND BIOGRAPHY

¶ This grading, which is simply suggestive, represents the earliest years in which these books can be read to advantage.

YEAR

5	Arnold's Stories of Ancient Peoples	$0.50
5	Baldwin's Abraham Lincoln	.60
5	Conquest of the Old Northwest	.60
5	Discovery of the Old Northwest	.60
4	Four Great Americans . . . .,	.50
4	Beebe's Four American Naval Heroes	.50
4	Burton's Four American Patriots	.50
5	Story of Lafayette	.35
6	Clarke's Story of Caesar	.45
8	Cody's Four American Poets	.50
8	Four American Writers	.50
3	Dutton's Little Stories of France	.40
2	Eggleston's Stories of Great Americans for Little Americans .	.40
3	Stories of American Life and Adventure	.50
5	Guerber's Story of the Thirteen Colonies	.65
5	Story of the Great Republic	.65
5	Story of the English	.65
6	Story of the Greeks	.60
6	Story of the Romans	.60
6	Story of the Chosen People	.60
3	Horne and Scobey's Stories of Great Artists	.40
5	Kingsley's Four American Explorers	.50
5	Story of Lewis and Clark	.25
5	Perry's Four American Inventors	.50
5	Perry and Beebe's Four American Pioneers	.50
6	Pitman's Stories of Old France	.60
3	Scobey and Horne's Stories of Great Musicians	.40
3	Shaw's Discoverers and Explorers	.35
7	Van Bergen's Story of China	.60
7	Story of Japan	.65
7	Story of Russia	.65
5	Wallach's Historical and Biographical Narratives	.35
5	Whitney and Perry's Four American Indians	.50
5	Winterburn's Spanish in the Southwest	.55

AMERICAN BOOK COMPANY

THE AMERICAN WORD BOOK

By CALVIN PATTERSON, M.A.

· $0.25

A PROGRESSIVE and carefully developed plan for teaching the forms and values of English words in common use. The book begins with words illustrating the primary sounds, and printed both in Roman letters and in vertical script. These are followed by graded lessons on the different classes and uses of words.

¶ The lessons are made up of words often mispronounced, words of opposite meanings, words of several meanings, words in the possessive, words arranged topically, words pronounced alike but spelled differently, words spelled alike but pronounced differently, words defined, words in the singular and plural numbers, etc.

¶ There is also a series of lessons on punctuation and the use of capitals—subjects which are included naturally in a spelling book, but which in many schools do not receive attention sufficiently early.

¶ The selections for dictation have been carefully chosen from the best prose and poetry in literature. They can not fail to stimulate observation, and encourage a taste for good reading, and at the same time they lead to the accurate spelling of words, and to their correct use.

¶ The lessons are short, judiciously graded, and skillfully arranged. Special attention is devoted to the every-day words that give trouble in spelling, pronunciation, and correct use. New terms are introduced in connection with those already familiar.

¶ Diacritical marks are used just enough to prevent any mispronunciation, and to lead naturally to the intelligent use of the dictionary. The system of marks employed is that found in Webster's International Dictionary.

AMERICAN BOOK COMPANY

www.ingramcontent.com/pod-product-compliance
Lightning Source LLC
Chambersburg PA
CBHW020557270326
41927CB00006B/876